William Henry Bennett

The Theology of the Old Testament

William Henry Bennett

The Theology of the Old Testament

ISBN/EAN: 9783742810038

Manufactured in Europe, USA, Canada, Australia, Japa

Cover: Foto ©Lupo / pixelio.de

Manufactured and distributed by brebook publishing software (www.brebook.com)

William Henry Bennett

The Theology of the Old Testament

THE THEOLOGY

OF THE

OLD TESTAMENT

BY THE REV.

W. H. BENNETT, M.A.

Professor of Old Testament Languages and Literature, **Hack**
and New Colleges

NEW YORK
THOMAS WHITTAKER
2 AND 3, BIBLE HOUSE

PREFACE

SPECIAL difficulties beset the construction of a manual on any subject in which research is being vigorously carried on. Not only are new theories or discoveries constantly emerging, but old landmarks sometimes suddenly disappear. A text-book needs the advice:—

> "Be not the first by whom the new is tried,
> Nor yet the last to lay the old aside."

Yet the application of this precept is not easy. For instance, on page 97 it is said that the pronunciation of YHWH (*E.V.*,* "Jehovah") "is generally supposed to have been Yahweh," but since that page was written Mr. Pinches has announced that he has discovered that the true pronunciation of YHWH was Yahwah. As he gives no evidence it is hard to tell whether he has really solved this ancient enigma. Still, it is just possible that, before my little book is published, what has hitherto been generally held on this point may be as generally abandoned.

* *E.V.* is used for *A.V.* and *R.V.* where they agree.

But the difficulties arising from actual discoveries are slight compared with those caused by antagonistic theories. O. T. Theology must be based on that exegesis which recognises the results of textual, literary, and historical criticism. Each of these departments of O. T. study is the arena of fierce conflict. Points of detail and the general theory of O. T. are contested with equal enthusiasm.

The compass of this work excludes lengthy explanation and almost all argument. Hence it has been necessary to carefully limit the treatment of the subject. The ideal O. T. Theology would contain, in the first place, a history of the religion of Israel, expounding the teaching of Isaiah, Jeremiah, etc.; the characteristics of faith and worship in each period; and the sequence and relation of the successive unfoldings of divine truth. In the second place, it would attempt some general sketch of O. T. teaching, laying, however, the main stress on its historical aspect. It is just here that controversy rages most fiercely; opposing schools differ *toto cælo et orco* as to the date of some of the most important documents, and as to the character of the early history. The difficulty of expounding Isaiah will be obvious to any one who glances at such a table as that in Prof. Max Kellner's *Prophecies of Isaiah*, classifying the conclusions of Professors Cheyne, Cornill, Driver, and Kellner in their analyses of these prophecies. Here, therefore, I have been forced to confine the consecutive historical treatment to a single chapter—Chapter II., "Israel in History"—and have dealt very briefly indeed with the pre-prophetic period. In the periods treated in some detail, I have minimised the use of controverted data. It must be remembered that many O. T terms and practices, both secular and ritual alike, had their origin, not in Revealed Religion, but outside its circle, or before its beginnings, and therefore the primitive meaning of such terms and practices forms no part of O. T. Revelation. In the following chapters I have tried to give a general sketch of O. T. teaching, still tracing as far as possible the development of doctrine and the relation of each feature to the historic setting in which it appears.

Chapter V. "Israel as the People of Jehovah," needs, perhaps, a special explanation. In this I have to some extent combined features from the Levitical Law with the pictures of the Israel of the Monarchy. For I am convinced that in spite of much that is late in form and detail, and even in spirit—the Levitical Law, as well as Deuteronomy has a certain spiritual harmony with the prophetic ideal for Israel. Moreover, O. T. has come down to us as an integer, for which first the Jewish and then the Christian Church claimed integral authority. We are therefore bound to attempt some total estimate of its teaching.

From this standpoint, as well as for reasons of space, I have given no detailed separate treatment to the Law, the History, the Prophets, and the Wisdom, Apocalyptic, and Devotional Literature. Often they only represent contemporaneous aspects of the same religious movements.

A word may be added on some interesting questions which lie, for the most part, outside the strict limits of O. T. Theology. No sentence ever conveys exactly to a reader the meaning intended by its author, nor conveys exactly the same meaning to any two readers. Before the O. T. was complete its materials had passed through the hands of many editors, each of whom had understood with a difference, so that many sentences may be standing in canonical Scriptures, only in virtue of interpretations alien to the thought of the first author. This inspired process of progressive interpretation continued after the O. T. Canon was closed. A Jew of the time of Cyrus, and a Pharisee of the time of Christ must have held widely divergent views as to the resultant teaching of Isaiah or Jeremiah; and a Roman or Corinthian Christian at the end of the first century would have differed from them both even more widely still. Similarly, to determine what views of O. T. were held by the Apostles as Jews (before their conversion), and shared by them with their fellow-countrymen, has great importance for the history of Christianity; but none of these

PREFACE

questions strictly belong to O. T. Theology. Moreover, a Christian to-day naturally asks how N. T. interprets O. T., and how far it modifies or even supersedes its teaching. But the investigation of these problems belongs to N. T. Theology (cf. pp. 165-168).

A table is appended to show the broad divergence between the two leading schools of O. T. study, as to the dates of the books. Between the extreme limits almost every grade of opinion is held by one scholar or another. The table, which is intentionally made as general and elastic as possible, only represents approximately two dominant types of the opposing views. A is the view almost universally held before the middle of the last century. For the sake of clearness it is given in an extreme form: nearly all its modern adherents make considerable concessions to the school represented by Column B.

B is a form of the view now held by many of the most distinguished living O. T. scholars. Similar views are associated in England with the names of Professors Cheyne and Driver of Oxford, Professors Ryle and (the late) Robertson Smith of Cambridge, and Prof. G. A. Smith of Glasgow. Here again no attempt has been made in our table to follow these and other critics in their treatment of paragraphs and sentences as interpolations. The present work follows B, where it is necessary to decide between conflicting opinions.

In addition to the obligations mentioned in the

footnotes, I have made constant use of the works on O. T. Theology of Oehler and Schultz (Eng. Translations), Smend, and, in a less degree, Kayser (Marti's edition). Without attempting a bibliography, we may also refer the English reader to the standard commentaries on important passages; to the translation of Piepenbourg's *O. T. Theology*; and for information on special subjects and periods to Dr. Cave's *Inspiration of O. T.*, and *Scripture Doctrine of Sacrifice*, Dr. Cheyne's *Origin of the Psalter*, Dr. Duff's *O. T. Theology*, B.C. 800-640, Dr. James Robertson's *Early Religion of Israel*, the late Prof. Robertson Smith's *O. T. in the Jewish Church*, *Prophets of Israel*, and *Religion of the Semites*; and the portion of Dr. Salmond's *Christian Doctrine of Immortality*, which deals with O. T.

It is a matter of deep regret that Dr. A. B. Davidson's long-promised comprehensive work on this subject has not appeared in time to be made use of in this little manual. Dillmann's work was published since the following pages were printed.

I have again to acknowledge my great obligations to the Rev. T. H. Darlow, M.A., for a careful reading of the MS., and many valuable criticisms and suggestions.

December, 1895.

Period.	Books, etc., as to which there is Substantial Agreement as to Date.[*]	A.	B.
Before the Accession of Saul.		Job, Hexateuch, Psalm xc.	Sources of Parts of Hexateuch and Judges.
From the Accession of Saul to the Death of Solomon.		Judges, Ruth, 1 and 2 Samuel, Psalms, with titles David, Asaph, and Solomon, and others. Canticles, Ecclesiastes, and part of Proverbs.	Some Psalms? Part of Proverbs. Sources of Part of Samuel and Kings.
Death of Solomon to about Accession of Josiah.	Parts of Isa. i.-xxxix., Hosea, Amos, Micah (in part). Part of Proverbs. Some Psalms.	All Isaiah. All Micah. Joel, Jonah.	Prophetic documents of Hexateuch (JE), 1 and 2 Samuel. Joel? Canticles? Ruth? Zech. ix.-xiv.?
From about the Accession of Josiah to the Fall of the Monarchy.	Nahum, Zephaniah. Hababbuk. Parts of Jeremiah and Ezekiel.		Part of Deuteronomy. Part of Proverbs.
Exile.	Kings. Rest of Jeremiah and Ezekiel. Some Psalms. Lamentations, Obadiah.		Rest of Deuteronomy. Judges? Law of Holiness (H), Job? Part of Isa. xl.-lxvi., Part of Proverbs.
Persian Period.	Haggai, Zech. i.-viii., Malachi. Some Psalms.	Chronicles. Ezra. Nehemiah. Daniel, Esther. CLOSE OF THE CANON.	Most (?) of the Psalms. Priestly Code (P.). Parts of Isaiah and Jeremiah, Jonah, Joel? Canticles? Ruth?
Greek Period.			Chronicles, Ezra, Nehemiah, Zech. ix.-xiv.? Ecclesiastes.
Maccabæan Period.			Some Psalms. Daniel, Esther.

[*] This "substantial agreement" does not always extend to small sections of books, or to the form in which they are extant. In some cases it is doubtful in which of two successive periods a book should be placed. This also applies to A and B.

CONTENTS

DIVISION I
JEHOVAH AND ISRAEL

CHAPTER I

INTRODUCTION

		PAGE
§ 1.	The Old Testament: a Revelation in and through Israel.	3
§ 2.	Aspects of the Relation of Jehovah to Israel	3

CHAPTER II

ISRAEL IN HISTORY

§ 3. **Introductory**—i., History, a Revelation—ii., Starting Point—iii., Actual Life of Israel—iv., Twofold Judgment on that Life—v., Popular Judgment—vi., Judgment of the Prophets—vii. Prophetic Interpretation of History—viii., Application of the Teaching of History—ix., Elijah and Elisha . . 7

CONTENTS

§ 4. **Prophets of the Eighth Century**—i., Amos—ii., Hosea—iii. Isaiah's Call and Commission—iv., Isaiah's Message to Judah in the Reign of Ahaz—v., Isaiah and the War with Syria and Ephraim—vi., Isaiah and Israel—vii., Micah and Israel—viii., Fall of Samaria—ix., Micah and Judah—x., Isaiah and the Assyrians—xi., The Revolt against Assyria—xii., The Deliverance from Sennacherib—xiii., Hezekiah's Reformation **14**

§ 5. **The Publication of Deuteronomy**—i. Reaction under Manasseh and Amon—ii., Fall of Nineveh; Zephaniah, Nahum—iii., Publication of Deuteronomy; Josiah's Reformation—iv., Abolition of Idols—v., Suppression of High Places—vi., Priests of the High Places—vii., Prophets—viii., Other Ordinances, etc.—ix., Divine Unity—x., Doctrine of Forgiveness—xi., Beginning of the Canon **32**

§ 6. **Last Days of the Monarchy**—i., Megiddo—ii., Temple as Palladium—iii., Syncretism—iv., Jeremiah and the Last Kings of Judah—v., The Prophet as Traitor and Heretic—vi., The Inevitable Ruin of Judah—vii., The Remnant—viii., The Judgment of the Nations—ix., Habakkuk—x., Ezekiel and the Palestinian Jews—xi., Fall of Jerusalem—xii., Jewish Refugees in Egypt—xiii., Obadiah **43**

§ 7. **The Captivity**—i., Religion a Spiritual Life and not a Ritual Observance—ii., Literary Activity—iii., Formation of Ritual Codes—iv., Ezek., xl.-xlviii.—v., Law of Holiness, Lev. xvii.-xxvi —vi., Lamentations—vii., Isa., xl.-lxvi.—viii., Promise of Restoration—ix., Fall of Babylon and Return of the Jews **54**

§ 8. **Judaism**—i., The Restored Community and the Jewish Dispersion—ii., The Rebuilding of the Temple—iii., The Reforms of Ezra and Nehemiah; Levitical Law (Priestly Code); Malachi—iv., The Samaritans—v., Anti-legal Tendencies within Judaism; Ruth (?),

CONTENTS xv

Jonah (?), Proverbs, Job, Ecclesiastes, Psalms—vi., Divine Justice and the Sufferings of the Righteous; Job, Ecclesiastes—vii., Individualism—viii., Antagonism of Judaism and the Gentile World; Esther—ix., Persecutions of Antiochus Epiphanes; Daniel . 62

CHAPTER III

THE IDEAL ISRAEL

§ 9. **The Kingdom**—i., Messianic Prophecies—ii., Preparation for the Kingdom—iii., The Day of Jehovah—iv., The New Israel—v., Palestine as the Home of the New Israel—vi., The Constitution of the New Israel—vii., Moral and Spiritual Perfection—viii., The New Covenant—ix., Israel and the Heathen—x., Religious Supremacy of Israel—xi., The Kingdom of God 79

§ 10. **The Messiah**—i., Messiah as King—ii., Messiah as Prophet—iii., Messiah as the True Israel—iv., Messiah as Priest 87

§ 11. **New Heavens and New Earth** . 94

CHAPTER IV

JEHOVAH AS THE GOD OF ISRAEL

§ 12. **Names** 97

§ 13. **Anthropomorphism and Anthropopathism** . . 99

§ 14. **The Bond between Jehovah and Israel**—i., Election and Divine Sovereignty—ii., Providence—iii., Fatherhood—iv., Marriage—v., Israel the Client of Jehovah—vi., Covenant 100

§ 15. **Moral Attributes of Jehovah**—i., Trustworthiness and Self-consistency—ii., Benevolence—iii., Justice—iv., Glory, Majesty, Sanctity—v., The Name . . 103

§ 16. **Jehovah's Revelation of Himself**—i., Theophanies
—ii., Supernatural Organs: Spirit, Word, Wisdom,
Angels—iii., Transcendentalism—iv., Foreshadow-
ings of the Doctrine of the Trinity—v., Nature and
History—vi., Human Agents: Nation, King, Prophet,
Priest—vii., Methods—viii., Record—ix., Scope   . 105

CHAPTER V

ISRAEL AS THE PEOPLE OF JEHOVAH

§ 17. **Sanctity** 123
§ 18. **Sacred Places**—i., The Land of Israel—ii., Tenure
of Land—iii., High Places—iv., Cities of Refuge—
v., Tabernacle and Temple—vi., Synagogues . . 124
§ 19. **Sacred Persons**—i., Nation—ii., Royal Dynasty and
King—iii., Levites—iv., Priests—v., High Priests—
vi., Graduated Sanctity—vii., Representation of
Israel to Jehovah—viii., Prophets—ix., Seers, Sons
of the Prophets—x., Remnant—xi., Nazirites—
xii., Scribes 128
§ 20. **Sacred Seasons**—i., Sanctity of All Time—
ii., Agricultural Feasts—iii., Historical Feasts—
iv., Astronomical Feasts—v., Day of Atonement . 136
§ 21. **Sacred Acts**—i., Connected with the Land—
ii., Connected with the People—iii., Connection of
Sacred Acts with Sanctuaries, Feasts, and Priesthood—iv., Sacrifices—v., Ritual of Passover and
Day of Atonement—vi., Other Forms of Worship—
vii., Fasts—viii., Dedication of Persons and Places
—ix., The Ban—x., Oaths. 141
§ 22. **Sacred Objects**—i., Clean and Unclean Things—
ii., Apparatus of Worship—iii., The Ark and the
Mercy Seat—iv., Most Sacred Objects . . . 156
§ 23. **The Sanctity of Israel** 159
§ 24. **Preservation and Renewal of Sanctity** . . 160
§ 25. **Doctrine of Sacrifice** 163

CHAPTER VI

JEHOVAH AND THE ISRAELITE

	PAGE
§ 26. The Nation and the Individual	171
§ 27. Individual Righteousness	173
§ 28. Sin	175
§ 29. Rewards and Punishments	176
§ 30. Forgiveness	177
§ 31. Spiritual Gifts	178
§ 32. Apparent Failure of Divine Justice	179
§ 33. Future Life	187

DIVISION II

GOD AND THE UNIVERSE

§ 34. Man	193
§ 35. Evil	196
§ 36. Material Universe	197
§ 37. Supernatural Beings	197
§ 38. Doctrine of God	199

DIVISION I

JEHOVAH AND ISRAEL

CHAPTER I

INTRODUCTION

CHAPTER I

INTRODUCTION

1. The Old Testament a Revelation in and through Israel.—The Old Testament is the record of the Revelation of God which He gave to mankind through the life and history of Israel. Such a Revelation was necessarily made, in the first instance, to Israel itself. The nation learnt to know God by its experience of His Providence and the teaching of His inspired representatives. Its religion was a sense and recognition of His relation to Israel; and its theology —as far as any explicit theology existed—was the theory and statement of that relation. The Divine Name, Jehovah (cf. § 12), constantly styled "the God of Israel," symbolises the relation between God and the Chosen People. As the recipient of this Revelation, Israel represents mankind, and the relation between Jehovah and Israel, is a type of the relation which should exist between God and man (cf. § 33). On the other hand, so far as Israel accepted and obeyed its special Revelation, it represented God to the world, and became the inspired teacher of His truth to mankind (cf. § 7, vii.).

2. Aspects of the Relation of Jehovah to Israel.— We shall consider the relation of Jehovah to Israel under four aspects : (i.) As set forth in the events of the history of Israel ; (ii.) In connection with the prophetic ideal for Israel—the Messianic Kingdom of God. On the basis of (i.) and (ii.) we shall construct, as far as the material admits of technical form, a formal statement of the O. T. doctrine of (iii.) Jehovah as the God of Israel. Then, as distinct from the Messianic Israel, we shall describe the actual Israel, so far as it was faithful to Jehovah ; the righteousness to which devout kings, prophets and legislators sought to make the nation conform ; (iv.) Israel as the People of Jehovah.

CHAPTER II

ISRAEL IN HISTORY

CHAPTER II

ISRAEL IN HISTORY

3. Introductory. i. THE HISTORY AS A REVELATION.—All sections of the O. T. agree in regarding the History of Israel as the special sphere of the working of the Divine Providence, and therefore as itself a Revelation of the will and character of Jehovah.

ii. THE STARTING POINT FOR THE STUDY OF THE HISTORY.— This is naturally found in the special relation between Jehovah and Israel which is taken for granted throughout the O. T. This relation is often accepted as a simple fact in the nature of things; but it is also explained as the result of the Divine Election (§ 14, i.) of Israel. This election or calling became effectual in the series of events which made Israel a nation, the emigration from Chaldea, the preservation of the people during their nomad life, and especially the deliverance from Egypt, the Exodus, and the conquest of Canaan. So Hosea xi. 1, "When Israel was a child, then I loved him, and called My Son out of Egypt"; in Jer. ii. 2 Israel is "espoused" to Jehovah in the wilderness; in Ezek. xx. 5, Jehovah "chose Israel . . . and made Himself known unto them in the land of Egypt.' Cf. Exod. iii. 13 (E), vi. 2 (P).

Similarly, the Davidic dynasty (1 Sam. xvi. 1; 2 Sam. vii.) and its royal city, Jerusalem (Ezek. xvi.), owe their pre-eminence to the Divine Election. Moreover the disruption of Israel into two kingdoms is also due to the set purpose of Jehovah (1 Kings xi., xii.).

Thus in Israel we have a people who owe their origin and the conditions of their national life to the action of the sovereign will of Jehovah.

iii. THE ACTUAL LIFE OF ISRAEL.—In spite of this exceptional relation to Jehovah, the history clearly shows that Ancient Israel—the Israel of the Judges and the Monarchy—never attained for any long period to any exceptionally high standard of moral and spiritual life. On the whole, the life of Israel does not seem to have been of a very different character from that of other nations; it resembled most closely that of the neighbouring henotheistic tribes of Moab and Edom. Possibly as time went on and Israel advanced in power and culture, and entered into wider international relations, it surpassed its neighbours in the vices peculiar to civilisation, and in its predilection for religious eclecticism. On the other hand, we cannot suppose that Israel was conspicuously and consciously worse than surrounding peoples.

iv. TWOFOLD JUDGMENT UPON THE LIFE OF ISRAEL. —When men began to reflect upon the moral quality of this national life, they raised one of the great problems of Israelite theology. That Jehovah was the God of Israel, and that Israel was the People of Jehovah, was a fundamental axiom with all Israelites, but controversy arose as to the application of this principle. How far was Jehovah satisfied with the actual life of Israel, what treatment did Israel deserve at His hands, and how was He likely to treat His People? To these questions two main answers were given—that of the inspired prophets, and that of the people and the religious teachers who were the mouthpieces of popular feeling.

v. THE POPULAR JUDGMENT.—The popular conscience was not aware that the national life was inconsistent with that mutual devotion of Jehovah and Israel (cc. iv., v.) which was generally regarded as a fundamental article of faith.

(a) *Conditions of Jehovah's Favour.*—As regarded the moral character of ordinary life average Israelites were content with the same imperfect compromise accepted elsewhere. They did not suppose that Jehovah's favour was dependent upon moral conditions; but expected that Jehovah would help His People, simply because they were His People.

(b) *Value of Ritual.*—Such inducement as Jehovah might require to help Israel was to be found in ritual, especially sacrifice. Sacrifice had a value in itself, apart from the conduct and character of the worshipper; its efficacy was supposed to depend on quantity and technique, and not on moral and spiritual significance (Isa. i.).

(c) *Character of Worship.*—They did not suppose that Jehovah required a purer, more seemly, more humane, more spiritual worship than Baal, Moloch, or Chemosh. They sought to gratify Him by idolatry, religious prostitution (Amos ii. 7), obscene rites and symbols, and human sacrifice, especially the sacrifice of children.

(*d*) *Confusion with " Other Gods."*—They thought to manifest their devotion to Jehovah by ascribing to Him the attributes, and worshipping Him with the titles, symbols and rites of the gods of neighbouring tribes (Hosea ii. Cf. v. 16).

(*e*) *Divided Religious Allegiance.*—The use of rites, etc., ordinarily associated with "Other Gods" practically involved the more or less explicit worship of these deities; without however, as a rule, any renunciation of the worship of Jehovah.

(*f*) *Jehovah Responsible for Disaster.*—They were inclined to account for national catastrophes, not by their own sin, but by the failure of Jehovah to care for His People, either through lack of power or of goodwill. Hence they found a justification either for abandoning Him altogether, or at any rate for seeking further divine aid from other gods. Thus the Jewish refugees in Egypt, after the fall of Jerusalem, attributed their misfortunes to the wrath of the Queen of Heaven, against whom, apparently, Jehovah had been powerless to protect them (Jer. xliv.).

(*g*) *The Fate of Israel.*—Until, however, the final catastrophe of Judah, the Israelites clung to the hope that the Divine Favour guaranteed the prosperity and permanence of Israel, without reference to the moral and spiritual character of the national life. The "Day of Jehovah" was at hand, in which He would deliver His People.

(*h*) *The Character of Jehovah.*—It will thus appear that the Israelites generally had no clear understanding of the fact that Jehovah was a moral being. They did not recognise Him as unique or even supreme, but tended to confuse Him and even to put Him on a level with the tribal and national deities of their heathen neighbours.

vi. THE JUDGMENT OF THE PROPHETS.—The prophets confronted this popular theology with an emphatic and sweeping condemnation, and announced a different standard of conduct.

(a) *Conditions of Jehovah's Favour.*—The favour of Jehovah was not the indiscriminate indulgence shown by a foolish father to a spoiled child, but was based upon a covenant (§ 14, vi.), the terms of which were essentially moral.

(b) *Value of Ritual.*—Ritual, however splendid or profuse, was an abomination to Jehovah when offered by an immoral people. "To what purpose is the multitude of your sacrifices unto Me? saith Jehovah. I am full of the burnt-offerings of rams and the fat of fed beasts; and I delight not in the blood of bullocks, or of lambs, or of he-goats. ... Bring no more vain oblations; incense is an abomination unto Me; new moon and sabbath, the calling of assemblies. I cannot endure iniquity and the solemn meeting" (Isa. i. 11, 13. Cf. context).

(c) *Character of Jehovah and of Acceptable Worship.*—Jehovah was essentially different in His righteousness and His claims from all other gods. He must not be worshipped with the cruel and impure rites of heathen ritual; He must not be confounded with other gods, neither will He submit to share with them His sanctuaries, His land, or His people.

(d) *They declared that this standard was not observed.* —The solemn and unanimous judgment of the prophets pronounced that Israel had altogether failed to observe the conditions of the covenant between itself and Jehovah. Its life and worship were alike immoral.

(e) *The fate of Israel.*—Hence this covenant became void by Israel's default and wrongdoing; Israel had forfeited all claim on Jehovah's favour, and was liable to His wrath and vengeance. Therefore its special relation to Jehovah became the ground for inflicting a more severe punishment. " You only have I known of all the families of the earth, therefore I will punish you for all your iniquities " (Amos iii. 2). The sin of Israel was such that it was a moral impossibility for Jehovah to tolerate the continued existence of the nation; its ruin was inevitable; the "Day of Jehovah" would bring to Israel not deliverance but destruction. "Woe unto you that desire the day of Jehovah! Wherefore would ye have the day of Jehovah? It is darkness and not light " (Amos v. 18).

viii. THE PROPHETIC INTERPRETATION OF HISTORY. —Recognising the continuity of the national life of Israel, the prophets saw, in the former calamities of the people, divine judgments upon national sin. On the other hand, periods of prosperity were the reward of closer approximation to the true standard of life. This view is specially taught in the Book of Judges, which received its present form from editors who wrote under the influence of the teaching of the prophets. Throughout this book, as the people alternate between "doing evil in the sight of Jehovah" and "crying unto Jehovah," they are "sold into the hand of their enemy" and "delivered." We must, however, be careful to remember that supreme acts of the Divine Providence, such as the Exodus and the Conquest, are never considered as rewards for any righteousness of Israel.

viii. APPLICATION OF THE TEACHING OF HISTORY.— Certain elementary truths of O. T. Revelation were involved in this teaching :

(a) Sin brought suffering.

(b) A righteous life brought prosperity.

(c) The vicissitudes of the fortunes of Israel, the fact that the punishment even of gross national sin came to an end, that Israel survived, and was permitted to enter upon new periods of prosperity, showed that Jehovah forgave sin on condition of repentance and amendment.

The judgment of the prophets upon Israel and Judah, and their teaching generally, are largely the application of these truths to the life of their times.

ix. ELIJAH AND ELISHA.—These prophets were the forerunners of those whose writings still survive. Their mission was to assert the exclusive claims of Jehovah as against Baal. The people halted between two opinions—*i.e.*, they wished to worship Jehovah *and* Baal, or to have a worship which might serve indifferently for either. Elijah demanded that they should recognise that the two divine names represented two incompatible religious systems. The people could not combine them, they could not use now one and now another to suit changing circumstances, or to gratify a love of variety, they must make a definite and final choice between them. "How long halt ye between two opinions? If Jehovah be God, follow him: but if Baal, then follow him" (1 Kings xviii. 21). As the house of Omri specially favoured the combination of Baal worship with the pure worship of Jehovah, the controversy resolved itself into a contest between that dynasty and the prophets. In the end, Elisha overthrew the House of Omri, and raised Jehu to the throne. Henceforth the royal authority was exerted against Baal worship, and so far victory rested with the prophets. But such external revolutions did comparatively little to change the mind and habits of the people; and the accession of Jehu was only one stage in a long struggle.

4. **Prophets of the Eighth Century.** i. AMOS, cir. 750 B.C.—Nevertheless the history of the House of Jehu seemed to indicate that Jehovah was rewarding Jehu's action as acceptable service to Himself. Elisha supported the new dynasty by his counsel and encouragement, and by the weight of his prophetic authority; and Jeroboam II. brought the long duel between Samaria and Damascus to a successful close, and reigned for forty-one years with a splendour and power that recalled the days of David and Solomon. The Book of Kings tells us (2 Kings xiv. 23-27) Jeroboam II. was sent by Jehovah to save Israel according to the word of the prophet Jonah ben Amittai.

At this crisis, the first of the great prophets of the eighth century appeared upon the scene, and, possibly because he felt that his message constituted a new departure in the history of prophecy, he expressly defined the position and claims of a true prophet. He did not speak as a member of any established order, or in virtue of any special training or personal genius, or as having been charged with the transmission of any traditional teaching; but because he had received a direct and personal call from Jehovah: "I was neither a prophet, nor a disciple of the prophets; but I was a herdman, and a dresser of sycamore trees: and Jehovah took me from following the flock, and Jehovah said unto me, Go, prophesy unto My people Israel" (vii. 15). Such prophets—as distinguished from the mere professional preachers with whom Amos repudiated all connection—were admitted to full and intimate knowledge of the purposes of Jehovah. "Surely the Lord Jehovah will do nothing without revealing His secret unto His servants the prophets" (iii. 7). This Revelation is a trust for Israel. Jehovah is entirely frank and open in His dealings with His people. "Necessity is laid upon" the prophet to declare the secret plans of Jehovah to Israel. "The lion hath roared, who will not fear? The Lord Jehovah hath spoken, who can refrain from prophesying?" (iii. 8).

Under the stress of this divine compulsion, sustained by the consciousness of a supreme inspiration, Amos, the herdman of Tekoa in Judah, appeared at the royal sanctuary at Bethel to deliver his message. The Northern Kingdom was exulting in the glory and prosperity to which it had been raised by its victorious king. These blessings were received as tokens of divine favour and approval, as fresh evidence that the interest of Jehovah in His People guaranteed the safety and welfare of Israel. Amos, as the first spokesman of the New Prophecy, in the name of Jehovah repudiated once for all this ancient doctrine, and declared " Jeroboam shall die by the sword, and Israel shall surely be led away captive out of his land" (vii. 11). Elsewhere in his book this sentence is repeated and amplified. The divine displeasure had already been intimated by drought, failure of crops, famine, pestilence, and earthquake; these were calls to repentance, to which the people had turned a deaf ear (iv. 6-11). Therefore a day of distress and defeat (ii. 13-16, iii. 14, 15, iv. 12, v. 16-27, etc.) will come upon Israel, and they shall go into captivity beyond Damascus.

The recent victories of Israel had not really been due to renewed national vigour. Damascus had fallen because its strength had been worn away by the continual attacks of the Assyrians. For the moment the Assyrians had paused in their advance westward, and the fruit of their many campaigns had been gathered by Israel. But the fall of Damascus laid Israel bare to its new and more terrible enemy. Amos claimed this heathen empire as the instrument chosen by Jehovah to chastise His People. "Behold I will raise up a nation, that shall afflict you from the entering in of Hamath unto the brook of Arabah" (vi. 14). Jehovah had not merely ceased to be the Champion of Israel, but had armed her enemies against her. Amos dwells upon the sins which have drawn down this condemnation upon Israel; these are: the oppression of the poor by the rich and powerful (iii. 10, iv. 1, vii.); the venality of the judges and rulers (ii. 6); dishonest business dealings (viii. 5); impure worship (ii. 7).

In spite of their sins, the people thought to render themselves acceptable to Jehovah by innumerable sacrifices and offerings at their many sanctuaries (iv. 4, 5); but Jehovah repudiated and condemned their worship: "I hate, I despise your feasts, and I will take no delight in your solemn assemblies. Yea, though you offer me your burnt offerings and meat offerings I will not accept them; neither will I regard the peace offerings of your fat beasts" (v. 21, 22).

Not only the worship, but the sanctuaries are condemned. Here first we meet with that attack upon the high places which is one of the main features of the prophetic movement of the eighth century. Bethel, Gilgal, Beersheba, Dan, and Samaria are in turn denounced (iii. 14, iv. 4, 5, v. 5, viii. 14).

Judah is dealt with very briefly and generally. Amos, indeed, sees in Jerusalem the special dwelling-place of Jehovah. "Jehovah shall roar from Zion, and utter His voice from Jerusalem" (i. 2); but Jehovah saith also that, because Judah has disobeyed Him, He "will send a fire upon Judah, and it shall devour the palaces of Jerusalem" (ii. 5).

ii. HOSEA, cir. 735.—The death of Jeroboam II. was shortly followed by the overthrow of his dynasty. Torn by intestine strife and exposed to Assyrian invasions the country rapidly sank into misery and corruption. In the time of Amos the moral rottenness of the people had been partly hidden by a veneer of order and decency; but now, in the death throes of Israel, sin was manifest in open, highhanded crimes. Hosea had painful experience of the corruption of his times, not only as an Israelite, but also in his personal life; his prophetic mission and even the form of his message were conditioned by the adultery of his wife.

Similarly, Israel had been unfaithful to her husband Jehovah; whom she had confounded with (ii. 16), and forsaken for (ii. 5), Baal and Baalim. This unfaithfulness had led to gross wickedness: "There is no truth, nor mercy, nor knowledge of God in the land. There is nought but swearing and breaking faith, killing and stealing and committing adultery" (iv. 1, 2). The priests murder in the way toward Shechem, (vi. 9). The traders use deceitful balances (xii. 7).

The people still delighted in sacrifices and religious observances (ii. 11, iv. 13, viii. 11, x. 1); but their worship was impure (iv. 13); idolatrous (iv. 17, viii. 4, xiii. 2)—Baal-worship, though offered to Jehovah (ii. 13).

The high places are denounced (iv. 13), Gilgal (iv. 15, ix. 15. xii. 11), Gilead (xii. 11). The worship of the calf at Bethel (called in contempt Bethaven) is specially attacked (iv. 15, viii. 5, 6, x. 8, x. 15). Israel sought to conciliate Jehovah by splendid sanctuaries, countless altars (viii. 11) and sacrifices. Over against this trust in ritual Jehovah sets His demand for righteousness: "I desire mercy and not sacrifice; and the knowledge of God more than burnt offering" (vi. 6, viii. 13).

Besides ritual, Israel still trusted in his own power, in his chariots and the multitude of his warriors (x. 13); he had forgotten his Maker and built palaces (viii. 14).

If ritual and military power were insufficient, recourse was had to foreign allies, Egypt and Assyria (vii. 11). Hosea strikes another keynote of subsequent prophecy in his denunciation of these alliances.

In complete accordance with his use of the figure of marriage to illustrate the relation between Jehovah and Israel, he speaks of a covenant between God and His People (vi. 7, viii. 1). This covenant they have transgressed by choosing kings and rulers without seeking divine counsel (viii. 4), and by entering into a covenant with Assyria (xii. 1). Even the monarchy itself seems to be condemned as an ungodly institution (viii. 4, 10, xiii. 10, 11), and the sin and ruin of Israel are dated from "the day of Gibeah" when Saul was inaugurated as the first king of Israel * (ix. 9, x. 9. Cf. 1 Sam. x. 26, xi. 4, xii. 12, 13).

In accordance with the general teaching of the O. T. as to the close connection between folly and wickedness, Hosea attributes much of the sin of Israel to its indifference to the knowledge of God, which it had had every opportunity of attaining. "I have hewed them by the prophets; I have slain them by the words of My mouth: and My (R. V. Mg.) judgment goeth forth as the light. For I desire . . . the knowledge of God" (vi. 5, 6). "I wrote for him the ten thousand things of My law, but they are counted as a strange thing" (viii. 12. Cf. iv. 6).

* Smend, 194.

Because of this sin and wilful ignorance, Jehovah would renounce and ruin Israel. To symbolise this judgment, Hosea named his children "Lo-ruhamah" (Unpitied), and "Lo-ammi" (Not my people). Israel would be overthrown by Assyria, and carried captive to Assyria and Egypt (vii. 16, ix. 3, xi. 5). Yet even now Jehovah shows His fatherly affection (xi. 2) for Israel by His reluctance to punish and His yearning to forgive (xi. 8, 9; xiv.). While Amos sees no future hope for Israel, Hosea looks forward to a restoration of his people in righteousness and prosperity (i. 10, ii. 14-23, iii. 5, xiv.).

Judah is only dealt with in casual references.*

iii. Isaiah's Call and Commission.—Though Amos belonged to Judah, his message was almost entirely addressed to Israel. Isaiah is, in the strict sense, the first great prophet of Judah. His early life, before and at the beginning of his ministry, was spent in the prosperous days of Uzziah and Jotham, when Judah shared the renewed prosperity of Israel. His call (vi.) shows that, like Amos, he received the revelation that Judah was unclean—*i.e.*, failed to attain the divine standard set by Jehovah for the life of His people, and that this uncleanness alienated Jehovah from Judah. When experience had shown how little his ministry could do to change the character of the people, he realised that his appeals for repentance and amendment had only hardened their hearts, filled up the measure of their iniquity, and so sealed their doom. Here, therefore, we meet with another important feature of the prophetic teaching

* Often supposed to be editorial additions.

of this period—its conviction that the nation, as a whole, was incapable of any radical reformation, and that therefore its ruin was inevitable. Chapter vi. concludes with the introduction of another great prophetic doctrine which somewhat relieves the gloom —the doctrine of the Remnant. The nation may be hardened, and its case hopeless, but individuals will hear and obey, and these will form a community, which is the Remnant of the Old Israel and the seed of the New. Thus chapter vi. contains a brief statement of the main elements* of Isaiah's teaching. We have still, however, to notice how these were developed in the course of his career.

iv. Isaiah's Message to Judah in the Reign of Ahaz, b.c. 735.—The picture drawn by the Jewish prophets of the moral and religious state of Judah is not essentially different from the account given of Israel by Amos and Hosea. Isaiah charges the Jews with oppression and venality on the part of judges and rulers (i. 21-23, iii. 14, 15, v. 7, 23, x. 1-4); unscrupulous avarice (v. 8); pride (ii. 11, v. 21); immoral casuistry (v. 20); presumptuous and defiant sin (v. 18, 19); and drunkenness (v. 22). He specially charges the women with proud and wanton luxury (iii. 16). Judah is a "sinful nation, a people laden with iniquity, a seed of evil-doers, children that deal corruptly" (14).

In Judah, as in Israel, the people delight in profuse ritual, and hope thereby to conciliate Jehovah, but He rejects their sacrifices as worthless, an

* For the stress laid upon the character of Jehovah as *Qadosh*, E.V. "Holy," see §§ 17 *ff.*

intolerable abomination (i. 10-17). As the religious observances with which Isaiah was most familiar were those of the Temple, he naturally does not refer to the high places; except by implication in stating that "the land is full of idols" (ii. 8); and in speaking of the worship under oaks and in gardens (i. 29). Their superstition, however, had gone beyond trust in ritual; they delighted also in magic and divination; "they be filled with customs from the East, and are soothsayers like the Philistines" (ii. 6, viii. 19).

Isaiah announces "the day of Jehovah," His judgment upon these sins. "He has forsaken His people" (ii. 6). All their glory and pride shall be laid low (ii. 6-22). "Jerusalem is ruined and Judah is fallen" (iii. 8). Jehovah's vineyard shall be trodden down and laid waste: "it shall not be pruned nor hoed; but there shall come up briers and thorns: I will also command the clouds that they rain no rain upon it" (vii. 6). The instrument of this judgment will be "the nations from afar" (v. 26).

Isaiah, however, does not merely deal with the nation as a whole; he personally threatens special classes of society, the rulers (i. 23) and noble ladies (iii. 16—iv. 1); and special types of sinners, drunkards, etc. (v. 8-25). We have here a step towards the treatment of religion as regards the individual.

The alienation between Jehovah and Israel is consciously felt, and has become matter for discussion. Heaven and earth are called upon to hear Jehovah's charges against His people (i. 2), and the inhabitants of Jerusalem and Judah are appealed to to judge between Jehovah and His vineyard (v. 4). Yet

Jehovah Himself is the Judge (iii. 13). In "that Day," when all sinful splendour and pride is laid low, He alone is exalted (ii. 11). He first manifested Himself to Isaiah as the Divine King in His Heavenly Temple, surrounded by His angelic court of Seraphim, who hailed Him as the unique and supreme God (*Qadosh*, see §§ 17 ff.).

v. Isaiah and the War with Syria and Ephraim (vii.-ix.).—In Isa. i.-vi. the prophet, like Amos and Hosea, concerns himself chiefly with the moral and religious state of his country. In the following chapters he appears as the successor of Elisha; a statesman as well as a prophet, taking his place by the side of the king, and seeking to direct him in the details of his foreign policy. In view of the growing pressure of Assyria upon the Syrian states, Rezin, king of Damascus, and Pekah, king of Israel, sought to compel Ahaz to enter into a league to resist the common enemy. Ahaz refused, and sought the aid of Assyria against Rezin and Pekah.

Isaiah had already given striking expression to his doctrine of the Remnant, by naming his son Shear-jashub (a remnant shall return). When Ahaz was preparing for the war with Syria and Samaria, Isaiah went to meet him, accompanied by Shear-jashub, whose presence would be symbolical, and bade the king: "Take heed to be quiet"—*i.e.*, abstain from foreign alliances—and Jehovah would destroy Rezin and Pekah. He offered Ahaz any sign he chose to ask for. Ahaz refused to ask for a sign; whereupon Isaiah declared that the sign should be that when a maiden already pregnant should bear a son, the Divine Presence should have been so fully manifested that she might call him Immanuel (God with us); and that, before he was weaned—*i.e.*, within two or three years—both Rezin and Pekah should be slain (vii. 14-16); nevertheless, Judah itself should be wasted and desolate, so that the child must eat "butter and honey."

Ahaz, however, persisted in his alliance with Assyria, and Isaiah announced the devastation of the country by Egypt and Assyria, especially Assyria (vii. 17-25, viii. 8). Nevertheless, when about this time another son was born to Isaiah, he gave him the symbolic name of Maher-shalal-hash-baz (booty hastens, spoil speeds), in token that, before the child could talk, Damascus and Samaria would be spoiled by the king of Assyria (viii. 1-4).

The absence of any wide response to Isaiah's teaching and the failure of his protest against the Assyrian alliance taught him that the alienation between Jehovah and Judah meant hostility between prophet and people. His conduct and ideals must contradict theirs (viii. 11-13), and the God who was his Inspirer was a stumbling block and a snare to his hearers (14). For the present his warnings and teachings were to be a sealed book to them, but he would " wait on Jehovah " (viii. 16, 17).

Yet the Remnant had begun to form itself; Isaiah and his children were signs and wonders in Israel (viii. 18), and he had made disciples. Moreover, some prospect of deliverance might be discerned beyond the impending calamities; the day of Immanuel was at hand (vii. 14, viii. 8), when a worthy son of David

(ix. 2-7) should reign over a redeemed and purified Jerusalem (i. 25-27. Cf. iv.).

vi. ISAIAH AND ISRAEL.—In dealing with the fortunes of Judah when attacked by Rezin and Pekah, Isaiah had necessarily announced the fate of Israel—namely, its overthrow by Assyria (vii. 8, 16, viii. 4). Moreover, Isaiah, like all the prophets, regarded Israel and Judah as a religious and national unity; and he constantly groups them together in his sentence of doom. The barren vineyard, which is to be laid waste, is "the house of Israel and the men of Judah" (v. 7); Jehovah is a "stone of stumbling and a rock of offence to both houses of Israel" (viii. 14). But Isaiah also deals separately with the Northern Kingdom. In xxviii. 3-8, he describes how Ephraim—priests, prophets, and people—had fallen into sin and folly through drunkenness; wherefore, "The crown of pride of the drunkards of Ephraim shall be trodden under foot" (xxviii. 3). A similar threat of coming ruin to Israel is contained in xvii. 1-11; where, apparently, the doctrine of the Remnant is applied to the Northern Kingdom (xvii. 6).

vii. MICAH AND ISRAEL, before B.C. 722.—In accordance with the heading, which describes the book as: "The word of Jehovah which came to Micah concerning Samaria and Jerusalem," Micah's utterances concerning the two kingdoms are very closely combined, and his treatment of them is very similar; but it will be convenient to consider his teaching as to Israel, first, as part of the prelude to the Fall of Samaria; and to defer his words on Judah till after that event, and to take them as part of the prophetic preparation for the great deliverance from Sennacherib. Micah agrees with the other prophets in his picture of the social, political, and religious corruption of Israel (i. 6, 7, ii. 1-6, iii.), but deals with the subject more briefly and generally. He announces the imminent and utter ruin of Samaria: "I will make Samaria as an heap of the field, and as the plantings of a vineyard" (i. 6).

viii. THE FALL OF SAMARIA, B.C. 722.—The course of history after the death of Jeroboam II. followed the lines indicated by the prophets. The attack of Rezin and Pekah upon Judah collapsed through the interference of Assyria, and Judah was delivered after enduring much misery. First Damascus, and then Samaria, was conquered by the Assyrian, and the Syrian and Israelite population carried away into captivity. This series of events is of supreme significance for the religion of Israel. It confirmed in many ways the teaching of the prophets, and established the authority of Isaiah, their great living representative. It discredited the ancient doctrine of a bond between Jehovah and Israel, which guaranteed the inviolability of the Sacred Land and the Chosen People. Hitherto, as the usage of the word Israel implies, the Northern Kingdom had stood for Israel, both in political power and religious importance. Judah had no prophets like Elijah and Elisha; the first decisive victory of Jehovah over Baal was won at Jezreel, not at Jerusalem. Thus, in a sense, the overthrow of Samaria was the ruin of Israel, of the Chosen People of Jehovah. If the ancient doctrine had still prevailed, according to which the glory and existence of Jehovah were bound up with those of Israel, Jehovah must have perished with His People. But the teaching of the prophets had made it possible to believe in Jehovah even when Israel was destroyed. The great catastrophe happened in accordance with, and not in spite of, the Divine Purpose: it was proof, not of His impotence, but of His power. Moreover, Jehovah can not merely use His own people to defeat and subdue other nations; He can also use Assyria and Egypt to punish Israel. He is, therefore, Lord of all nations. Thus the Fall of Samaria breaks the ancient theory of the relation between Jehovah and Israel, and marks the first step towards a universal and individual religion.*

ix. MICAH AND JUDAH.—The attention of the prophets was now concentrated upon Judah; they pointed to the fate of Samaria as an awful warning to the Southern Kingdom. Micah describes the sin of Judah in similar terms to the other prophets, and announces the impending ruin of Jerusalem in words partly identical with those he had used of Samaria. "Therefore shall Zion for your sake be plowed as a field, and Jerusalem shall become heaps, and the mountain of the house—the Temple—as the high places of a forest" (iii. 12). The doctrine of the restoration of the Remnant of Israel is found in ii. 12. Israel here probably includes both Israel proper and Judah. (Cf. iv. 5.)

x. ISAIAH AND THE ASSYRIANS, B.C. 722-701.— Under Ahaz, Judah had become a tributary of Assyria, and had procured its intervention, thus

* Smend, 160.

doing much to hasten the ruin of Samaria. The interests of Judah demanded that it should continue loyal to its suzerain. On the other hand, Hezekiah—who had now succeeded Ahaz—was exposed to many temptations to revolt. The neighbouring Syrian states sought to involve Judah in a confederacy against Assyria. Merodach-baladan, tributary king of Babylon, sought Hezekiah's aid against Sargon (xxxix.); and, above all, Egypt continually tried to stir up Judah and its neighbours against Assyria. Isaiah set himself to counteract these inducements: he rebuked Hezekiah for the favourable reception given to the Babylonian ambassadors (xxxix. 6, 7), and vehemently opposed any proposals for alliance with Egypt (xix., xx.). Their trust in the material strength of Egypt implied a lack of faith in Jehovah. "Woe to them that go down to Egypt for help, and rely on horses; and trust in chariots, because they are many, and in horsemen, because they are very strong, but they look not unto the Holy One of Israel, neither seek Jehovah. . . . Now the Egyptians are men, and not God: and their horses flesh, and not spirit" (xxxi. 1, 3). Their confidence in Egypt would merely betray them to their ruin. "When Jehovah shall stretch out His hand, both he that helpeth shall stumble, and he that is holpen shall fall, and they shall all fail together" (xxxi. 3).

Thus the objection to foreign alliances, which had led Isaiah to protest against the appeal of Ahaz to Assyria, was now applied to Egypt; and henceforth hostility to Egypt was an important element of prophetic teaching. There came to be two parties

ISRAEL IN HISTORY

in Jerusalem, the Egyptian party and the party of the prophets; and the opposition between the two was personal (xxii. 15-19), as well as political and religious.

For the present, however, the strength and salvation of Judah lay in repentance, in trust in Jehovah, and in rest and quietness (xxx. 15)—*i.e.*, in the quiet acceptance of present political condition by submitting to Assyria. For some years Isaiah succeeded in inducing Hezekiah to maintain this attitude. There is, however, no indication that Isaiah discerned any moral or religious improvement in the nation.

xi. THE REVOLT AGAINST ASSYRIA, B.C. 705.—At last, however, the temptation to revolt became too strong to be resisted. Under the united pressure of Egypt, a powerful combination of Syrian states, and the Egyptian party in Jerusalem, Hezekiah gave way and joined in the revolt against Assyria.

This rejection of Jehovah's counsel on the part of king and people revealed to Isaiah afresh the deep-seated corruption of Judah. Its sin would bring speedy chastisement: " Woe to Ariel, to Ariel, the city where David encamped. . . . I will distress Ariel, and there shall be mourning and lamentation " (xxix. i. 2). Its Egyptian allies would be useless: "The strength of Pharaoh shall be your shame, and the trust in the shadow of Egypt your confusion " (xxx. 3). Both Egypt and Judah would be overthrown and reduced to the last extremity of distress (xxxi. 3).

Nevertheless, in this last extremity Judah should be delivered; Jerusalem should not be taken by the invader, but a great calamity should fall upon Sennacherib, and send him home foiled and dishonoured (x. 24-34, xiv. 24-27, xxix. 1-8, xxx. 31-33, xxxi. 8, 9).

xii. THE DELIVERANCE FROM SENNACHERIB, B.C. 701.—Sennacherib advanced into Syria, overthrew the Syrians, defeated the Egyptians, ravaged Judah, and captured its fortresses. Hezekiah offered to submit, and complied with one demand after another, till at last he drew the line at the surrender of his capital, and stood at bay, encouraged by Isaiah's promises of deliverance. The deliverance came, the Assyrian army was smitten and destroyed by the Angel of Jehovah, and Sennacherib returned to Nineveh.

In its importance for the history of religion, this great deliverance ranks with the Exodus, the Conquest, and the Fall of Samaria. It confirmed afresh the authority of Isaiah and of the divine revelation given through the prophets. It secured a respite for Judah, during which true religion became too firmly rooted to be torn up and destroyed by the exile.

Like the other supreme interventions of Jehovah on behalf of His people, it is in no sense a reward of any righteousness of theirs : Isaiah does not connect it with Hezekiah's reformation. Jehovah defends the city, "for My own sake and for My servant David's sake" (xxxvii. 35). He also overthrows the Assyrian, because, though they were only the rod with which Jehovah chastised His People, they thought they had conquered in their own strength ; they became uplifted with pride, and even supposed they had overcome Jehovah as well as Judah (x. 5-16, xxxvi. 19, 20, xxxvii. 12-29. Jehovah thus manifested afresh His supremacy over the nations; the great empires were merely His weapons, which, when they ceased to serve His purposes, He destroyed and cast away.

xiii. HEZEKIAH's REFORMATION (2 Kings xviii. 4).— Isaiah would make use of his influence, not only to direct the politics of Judah, but also to raise its social and religious life. The time for which he had waited (viii. 17) had arrived, and no doubt his disciples (viii. 16) increased in number. There came to be an appreciable minority in Judah, who sought to live the higher life demanded by the prophets, and were helped to do so by Isaiah's teaching as to the nature and grace of Jehovah. Moreover, Isaiah was able in some measure, to carry out his views as to the externals of worship. The Book of Kings tells us that Hezekiah "removed the high places, brake the *Maççeboth*, cut down the Ashera, and brake in pieces the brazen serpent that Moses had made; for unto those days the Israelites burnt incense to it, and it was called Nehushtan." Nothing is said about the exact date of these proceedings, which may have been spread over a considerable period, perhaps over the whole of Hezekiah's reign. It is natural to suppose that they originated in the renewal of Isaiah's influence after the deliverance from Sennacherib; but even if they began earlier, that great event would rouse the king to new activity. The connection of this Reformation with Isaiah's teaching is best seen in the destruction of idols, of which Nehushtan may be taken as an illustration. Isaiah, following Amos (v. 26, and Hosea viii. 5, etc.), constantly denounces the use of idols (ii. 8, 18, etc.). The almost entire silence of Isaiah as to the high places, makes it improbable that Hezekiah's action against them was very persistent, and the account of the next reformation shows that he can only have been very partially successful in dealing either with high places or with idols (2 Kings xxiii. 4-14. Moreover, the reaction under Manasseh showed that Hezekiah's reformation had produced very little effect on Jewish minds generally. It was probably regarded as an innovation, and at the king's death his policy was reversed in an outburst of popular fanaticism. As Isaiah himself had foreseen, the permanent result of his work lay in the Remnant, the little band of believers which was slowly being gleaned out of the wreck of Jehovah's vineyard.

5. Publication of Deuteronomy. i. THE REACTION UNDER MANASSEH AND AMON (2 Kings xxi.).—Manasseh seems not merely to have reversed his father's policy and restored the ancient religious customs of Judah. He devoted himself with superstitious zeal to the cruel worship of Moloch, to whom he sacrificed his son. He practised a wider eclecticism than his predecessors, and even set up altars for "all the host of heaven" in the temple courts. His government seems to have been exceptionally bad, "He shed very much innocent blood, till he had filled Jerusalem from one end to the other" (xxi. 16). Political and religious partisanship were closely combined: the true prophets and their followers would denounce and oppose Manasseh; they were not likely to be spared when the king was shedding innocent blood in profusion. Thus at the very outset of its career, the Remnant was purified and strengthened by suffering and persecution. Later prophets saw in the crimes of Manasseh the unpardonable sin that ensured the ruin of Judah (Jer. xv. 4).

ii. ZEPHANIAH, cir. B.C. 630; NAHUM, cir. B.C. 625 (?). THE FALL OF NINEVEH.—During the minority of Josiah, the prophetic party regained their influence in the state. The violence and cruelty of Manasseh must have told in their favour: and in this period there was a fresh outbreak of prophetic activity, represented by the writings of Zephaniah, Nahum, Habakkuk, and some of the earlier prophecies of Jeremiah.

Zephaniah follows closely in the footsteps of Isaiah in his picture of the corruptions of Judah, and of the Day of Jehovah in which these corruptions shall be chastised. In this Day of Judgment, not only will Assyria (ii. 13) be overthrown, but Jehovah will pour out His fierce anger upon all the nations of the earth (iii. 8). There is to be a redeemed remnant of Judah (ii. 7, 9) and of Israel (iii. 13). These prophecies of judgment like those in Jer. i. 11-19, are often connected with the Scythian inroad, which devastated Western Asia in the early part of Josiah's reign.

Nahum exults over the impending ruin of Nineveh and the release of Judah from the Assyrian yoke. Nineveh perishes because it is morally corrupt, a "bloody city, all full of lies and robbery" (iii. 1), and because it is the "adversary of Jehovah" (i. 1)—*i.e.*, because it has oppressed Judah. Thus Nahum strikes an entirely different note to Isaiah and his followers. He has no message concerning the sin and doom of Judah, Assyria is not Jehovah's instrument in punishing the guilty, but is denounced as the wicked oppressor of His Chosen People. Instead of heralding judgment upon a nation whose insincere worship is rejected by Jehovah, Nahum cries: "Behold upon the mountains the feet of Him that bringeth good tidings, that publisheth peace! Keep thy feasts, O Judah, perform thy vows: for the wicked one—the Assyrian oppressor—shall no more pass through thee: he is utterly cut off" (i. 15). Nevertheless, Nahum agrees with the other prophets in this one essential point: that Nineveh is condemned, not merely or chiefly in the interests of Judah, but because it is itself morally corrupt.

In the early years of Josiah's reign the course of events was rapidly bringing about the fulfilment of these and previous prophecies. The Scythian inroad broke the strength of the Assyrian Empire, and though Nineveh itself does not seem to have been taken till about B.C. 605, yet its dominion was reduced to great straits some years before, and its ruin was obviously impending. Jehovah had justified the claim which the prophets had made on His behalf, that He was Lord of the lords and King of the kings of the world.

iii. THE PUBLICATION OF DEUTERONOMY AND THE REFORMATION OF JOSIAH, B.C. 621 (2 Kings xxii., xxiii.). —The weakness of Assyria allowed Judah to regain its independence, and to recover something of its old power and prosperity. Josiah even exercised some amount of sway over the former territory of Israel (xxiii. 15-20). The collapse of Assyria would confirm Josiah in his religious policy, and encourage him to renew Hezekiah's attempt to make Judah loyal to the will of Jehovah as revealed by His prophets. This new reformation was inaugurated by a covenant to observe the law as laid down in a roll discovered in the Temple while it was under repair in B.C. 621. This roll seems to have contained the "kernel of Deuteronomy"—*i.e.*, the laws, etc., of the central chapters of that book.

iv. THE ABOLITION OF IDOLS.—Josiah dealt with both the idols and the high places more thoroughly and—for the time at any rate—with more success than Hezekiah. Deuteronomy not only forbade "graven images" (*pesel*), (v. 8), but also the *maççebas* and *asheras* (xii. 3, xvi. 21, 22), and all worship of "other gods" (xiii. 1-8). Accordingly Josiah destroyed all the apparatus for such worship (2 Kings xxiii. 4-15).

v. THE SUPPRESSION OF THE HIGH PLACES.—The accounts of Manasseh's idolatry and Josiah's reformation show that in the matter of the use of idols and other corruptions of worship there was nothing to choose between the Temple and the high places. At the same time ritual purity could more easily be maintained at a single conspicuous sanctuary in the capital under the eye of the king and the prophets, than at a number of high places scattered through the country, some of which were probably the obscure homes of nameless abominations. Moreover, the limitation of sacrifice to a single sanctuary was an effectual check to the popular faith in a profusion of ritual. Such a limitation necessarily involved a reduction of the quantity of ritual, and tended to direct attention to its quality and spirit. Moreover, the course of events seemed to indicate a divine judgment on the high places, and a divine choice of Jerusalem and the central Temple. The high places of Samaria perished in the overthrow of Israel: those of Judah had suffered in the invasion of Sennacherib, while Jerusalem and the Temple had remained untouched. While the elder prophets never condemn the high places on the ground that the Temple was the only legitimate sanctuary of Jehovah, nevertheless they seemed to indicate a certain preference for the Temple. The preoccupation of Amos and Hosea with Israel prevented them from dealing with the corruption of the Temple; and though Micah announced the destruction of the Temple on account of the sins of the priests, prophets, and people of Jerusalem, no such definite condemnation of the Temple is found in any extant prophecy of Isaiah or Zephaniah. Moreover, the favourable attitude of the prophets toward the Temple is not merely shown by their comparative silence as to the corruptions of its worship. Though they say little of the Temple itself, the stress laid on Jehovah's connection with Jerusalem implies His special presence in its shrine. According to Amos i. 2, Jehovah roars from Zion, and utters His voice from Jerusalem. Isaiah prophesied the escape of Jerusalem from

Sennacherib, and even if the temple in Isa. vi. and Micah i. 2 meant originally Jehovah's heavenly house, these references would inevitably be understood of the Temple at Jerusalem. The origin and date of the prophecy which occurs both as Micah iv. 1-4, and as Isa. ii. 1-4, are too disputed to allow us to use it as evidence for this period, but it might serve to express the unique importance which the Temple was now acquiring.

Thus many influences—the course alike of history and revelation, the pride of Jerusalem in its Temple and of the king in his royal sanctuary—combined to facilitate the suppression of the high places, and the exaltation of the Temple as the only legitimate seat of sacrifice. As far as extant documents are concerned, the divine authority for this revolution is found, not in any prophetic utterance, but in Deut. xii. 1-16, xvi.—*e.g.*, xii. 13, 14: "Take heed to thyself that thou offer not thy burnt-offerings in every place that thou seest: but in the place which Jehovah shall choose in one of thy tribes—*i.e.*, the Temple at Jerusalem—there thou shalt offer thy burnt-offerings, and there thou shalt do all that I command thee."

Accordingly, Josiah "defiled the high places . . . from Geba to Beer-sheba; and brake down the high places of the gates that were at the entering in of the gate of Joshua, the governor of the city . . . and the high places in front of Jerusalem . . . which Solomon built for Ashtoreth . . . Chemosh . . . and Milcom . . . did the king defile . . . he brake down the altar and the high place at Bethel . . . and overthrew all the houses of the high places in the cities of Samaria" (2 Kings xxiii. 8, 13, 15, 20).

vi. THE PRIESTS OF THE HIGH PLACES.—The suppression of the high places deprived their numerous priests—*i.e.*, Levites—of employment and sustenance. Deuteronomy contains ordinances intended to provide for them. These Levites are recommended to the people as suitable objects of charitable hospitality (xii. 19, xiv. 27-29). Moreover, xviii. 6-8 directs that the country Levites—the priests of the high places—may come to Jerusalem and "minister in the name of Jehovah his God, as all his brethren the Levites do, which stand there before Jehovah. They shall have like portions to eat, beside that which cometh of the sale of his patrimony"—*i.e.*, the priests of the high places might claim to be admitted to all the rights and emoluments of the Temple priesthood. Naturally, such an arrangement would be very unwelcome to the priests of Jerusalem, and it was never carried out. Josiah slew the priests of the Israelite high places upon their own altars (2 Kings xxiii. 20); the priests of the Jewish high places were brought to Jerusalem and allowed to "eat unleavened bread among their brethren," but they were excluded from the priestly ministrations.

vii. THE PROPHETS (xviii. 15-22).—It is promised according to the request of the people at Horeb, that God will communicate His will to the people by prophets like Moses. The prophet that spoke without divine authority or in the name of other gods "shall die." The false prophet is known by the non-fulfilment of the predictions which he has uttered.

viii. OTHER ORDINANCES, ETC.—In other respects Deuteronomy partly reproduces and expands earlier (JE) codes and forms an intermediate stage in the transition from them to the Levitical Law. In accordance with the prophetic teaching, its aim throughout is to purify and limit ritual, and to promote honourable and generous dealings between man and man, and reverent and trustful loyalty towards God. One motive assigned for obedience is the divine election of Israel to be His special possession (*Sgulla*) a people consecrated (E.V. "holy") to Himself (vii. 6, xiv. 2, xxvi. 18, 19), a conception of the relation of Jehovah to Israel closely allied to that of the covenant (§ 14, vi.).

ix. THE DIVINE UNITY.—The leading features of Josiah's Reformation and of the teaching of Deuteronomy tend to emphasise and safeguard a faith in monotheism. The disuse of idols, *maççebas*, *asheras*, and other semi-heathen apparatus and ritual, drew a sharp distinction between Jehovah and "other gods," and effectually promoted obedience to the prophetic and Deuteronomic prohibition of the worship of "other gods." As in popular Romanism, the Virgin tends to be multiplied, so that Our Lady of one town is almost regarded as a separate personality from Our Lady of another; so the Baal of one shrine had come to be distinguished from the Baal of another and O.T. speaks of the Baalim. A similar multiplication of Jehovah might easily have taken place—*e.g.*, Jehovah Jireh might have been distinguished from Jehovah Nissi. The limitation of the worship of Jehovah to a single sanctuary was an effectual safeguard against this danger. One sanctuary, and one only, was a perfect symbol of the Divine Unity, a constant proclamation of the Deuteronomic watchword, "Jehovah our God, Jehovah is One" (vi. 4).

x. THE DOCTRINE OF FORGIVENESS.—A somewhat remarkable situation was created by the Covenant which adopted Deuteronomy as an inspired code for Judah. The reign of Manasseh and the early years of Josiah had been condemned by the prophets; Zephaniah and Jeremiah had declared in the beginning of Josiah's reign that Jehovah would visit Judah with condign punishment, if not with utter ruin. As yet, however, this punishment was in suspense. Moreover in 2 Kings xxii. 15-17, we read that, when Huldah the prophetess was consulted with regard to the threats in Deuteronomy, she replied: "Thus saith Jehovah, Behold, I will bring evil upon this place, and upon the inhabitants thereof, even all the words of the book which the king of Judah hath read, because they have forsaken Me, and have burned incense unto other gods, that they might provoke Me to anger with all the work of their hands; therefore My wrath shall be kindled against this place and it shall not be quenched."

Nevertheless, under the shadow of this sentence of doom, king and people entered into covenant with Jehovah, and proceeded to carry out their share of it with great zeal and energy. The editor of the Book of Kings declares that their devotion was futile, and almost implies that Jehovah met this covenant by an explicit announcement of the coming captivity.

ISRAEL IN HISTORY 41

We must remember, however, that the Book of Kings was compiled under the influence of the overwhelming impression made upon the Jewish mind by the destruction of Jerusalem and the Temple, and the exile of the People. Josiah's reign and all the events immediately preceding the Captivity are there described chiefly in their relation to the final catastrophe. This probably determined the selection of material for the Books of Kings and Jeremiah, as well as the point of view from which the editorial notes in the former book are written.

The attitude of contemporaries must have been different. Obviously the covenant and reformation would have been impossible, if the people had understood that their fate was sealed and their ruin inevitable. No explicit account has been preserved of the hopes and promises by which the covenant was accompanied; but there is much in the teaching of Jeremiah which may fairly represent them. Jeremiah (iv. 2, etc.) constantly promises forgiveness and deliverance, as the reward of repentance and amendment, such as this covenant symbolised. Neither are these promises always qualified by any statement that some measure of punishment must be endured before Judah can enjoy Jehovah's favour. The teaching, therefore, of Jeremiah, which is virtually assumed in Josiah's reforms, is that Jehovah meets and blesses the repentant sinner in the first moment of his repentance. Previous threats were conditional; they assumed that the sinner would persevere in his evil ways, and are therefore annulled by his penitence. Josiah—probably with the sanction, or even at the suggestion, of Jeremiah—instituted the covenant, in the hope that his reforms would be accompanied by national repentance and amendment, and would inaugurate a new era of national righteousness. Jeremiah, no doubt, assured the people that such a reformation would be accepted by Jehovah and would insure the safety and prosperity of Judah. The religious significance of these events is partly independent of their sequel. They involved a declaration of the divine willingness to forgive the repentant sinner, who is earnestly bent on amendment. Here, as elsewhere, the sinner is the nation; it is a question of national guilt and forgiveness; but the principle applies *mutatis mutandis* to the individual; though for the earliest application of it to the individual we must wait till a later stage in the history.

xi. THE BEGINNING OF THE CANON.—Though considerable portions of the O. T. existed before B.C. 621, yet Josiah's covenant marks the beginning of the O. T. Canon, in the sense that Deuteronomy was then, and has ever since been, recognised as an authoritative divine revelation. Hitherto the Torah, or revelation of the divine will, had been sought from the living words of priests and prophets; now it began to take the form of a written Law. For the present, however, the inspired prophet continued to exercise a much greater authority than the inspired writing. No prophet before Malachi (iv. 4) refers to the written Torah as an authority; though, possibly, the statement that Ezekiel (ii. 9, iii. 3) swallowed a roll symbolises his dependence on Deuteronomy. On the other hand the editor of the Book of Kings clearly recognises Deuteronomy as the standard of national life (2 Kings xviii. 6, xxiii. 25).

6. **The last Days of the Monarchy.** i. THE DISASTER OF MEGIDDO, B.C. 608.—For a while the prosperity of Josiah confirmed the authority of Jeremiah and Deuteronomy, and seemed to assure Judah that Jehovah had accepted the covenant, forgiven His people, and received them into His favour. But the revival of Jewish power through the weakness of Assyria soon came to an end. Babylon succeeded to the authority of Nineveh, while Pharaoh Necho, king of Egypt, sought to regain the ancient Egyptian dominion in Syria. Josiah, doubtless under the influence of the anti-Egyptian views of the prophets, sought to arrest Pharaoh's march to the Euphrates, but was defeated and slain at Megiddo. The anti-Egyptian party gave the throne to his son Jehoahaz; but Pharaoh soon appeared at Jerusalem, deposed Jehoahaz, and sent him captive to Egypt, and made his brother Jehoiakim king in his stead.

Hitherto the issue of the crises of Jewish history had confirmed the authority of the prophets; but the defeat at Megiddo threw everything into confusion. According to 2 Kings xxii. 20, Huldah had promised that Josiah should be gathered to his grave in peace; and yet the reforming king — of whom it is said that, " Like unto him there was no king before him, that turned to Jehovah with all his heart, and soul, and might, according to all the law of Moses; neither after him arose there any like him " (xxiii. 25) — was defeated and slain in the prime of manhood (at the age of 39), when he was obediently carrying out the anti-Egyptian policy of the prophets. Jehovah replied to the covenant and the reformation by making Judah the tributary of Egypt, under the rule of a nominee of Pharaoh.

The same logic, which saw in the deliverance from Sennacherib and the ruin of Assyria a confirmation of the teaching of Isaiah, interpreted the defeat of Megiddo as a divine repudiation of Josiah, Jeremiah, and Deuteronomy. The Egyptian, or anti-prophetic, party was installed in power at Jerusalem, and the religious life of Judah fell back into the old grooves, out of which Hezekiah and Josiah had tried to lift it.

ii. THE TEMPLE AS PALLADIUM.—This reaction claimed to be, what we should call in modern language, conservative and orthodox. It fell back on traditional teaching and restored ancient institutions, probably, for instance, the high places. Moreover, the reaction appropriated in some measure the prestige of Isaiah and the earlier prophets, and even succeeded in turning the results of Jeremiah's work against himself. The overthrow of Sennacherib and Isaiah's teaching had revived the old doctrine of the necessary relation between Jehovah and Israel. That great deliverance seemed to show that Jehovah had chosen Judah to be the true Israel, and meant henceforth to dwell in the Temple and protect Jerusalem from all its enemies. These ideas were confirmed by the unique importance which Deuteronomy and Josiah's reforms ascribed to the Temple. Popular superstition was only too ready to believe that the fate of Judah would depend, not on conduct and character, but on the magic value of the sacred building. The old faith in ritual, *quâ* ritual, revived in a new form and under new sanctions.

iii. SYNCRETISM.—At the same time the reversal of Josiah's policy involved the revival of other ancient corruptions of Jewish religion, especially the confusion of Jehovah with "other gods," and the worship of such gods. The disaster of Megiddo might be due to Jehovah's anger, that He was worshipped at fewer sanctuaries, and with simpler rites than Moloch or Chemosh. Or, if Jeremiah were right, and the simpler worship were the will of Jehovah, then clearly He was unable to protect His obedient servants, and it would be well to seek further divine aid. Accordingly, in the last days of the monarchy, the ancient Jewish love of Syncretism reasserted itself with fresh vigour, and the Jews did homage to the ancient deities of Canaan, to the new gods whose worship Manasseh had introduced, and probably to many others. Cf. Jer. xi. 28. "According to the number of thy cities are thy gods, O Judah"; the references to the worship of the "Queen of Heaven" (vii. 18, xliv.), and the account of Jewish cults in Ezek. viii. Moreover, as the fortunes of Judah became desperate, the Oriental predilection for magic and sorcery was indulged in more freely than ever.

iv. JEREMIAH AND THE LAST KINGS OF JUDAH, B.C. 608-586.—The fact that Jeremiah's confidence in his mission and message survived Megiddo is a remarkable proof of the power and tenacity of his inspired faith. Naturally, however, the popular interpretation of history was not accepted by Jeremiah and his friends. The disasters of Judah were not due to any divine displeasure with Josiah, but to the still unexpiated sins of Manasseh. Forgiveness was withheld from Judah, not because Jehovah disapproved of the Deuteronomic Reformation, but because the people had merely acquiesced in external reforms, and had shown themselves incapable of any heartfelt repentance or sincere effort after amendment. From this time till the end of his career Jeremiah continually reiterates the judgment, which the former prophets passed upon the life of Israel and Judah, and asserts with renewed emphasis and detail the social, moral and religious corruption of all classes in the nation.

We do not know how Jeremiah accounted for the untimely fate of Josiah. It was not till centuries later that the Chronicler (2 Chron. xxxv. 20-24.) ventured to sacrifice the character of Josiah to the necessities of Jewish dogmatism. In Jer. xxii. 15, 16, the prophet twice declares that "it was well" with Josiah. We could easily understand that to reign in prosperity and independence for thirty-one years, and then to die in battle *was* "well"; far better than to be like his successors, first the puppet and then the captive of foreign kings. But such views would be an anachronism if applied to the period of Jeremiah. Then it was believed that the final judgment of God upon a man's life might be gathered from the fortunes of his last days (Ezek. xviii.), and the fate of his children. According to both these tests Josiah stood condemned. Probably his career stimulated that discussion of the sufferings of the righteous, which culminates in Job and Isa. liii.

In any case, Jeremiah and his party never recovered from the blow dealt to them by the defeat at Megiddo. They still retained great influence, and struggled against the Egyptian and reactionary party with varying success; but they never regained that complete authority over the government and the people which they had enjoyed under Josiah.

The subjection of Judah to Egypt was speedily succeeded by its submission to Nebuchadnezzar; but Pharaoh's nominee, Jehoiakim, had sufficient address to retain his throne under the new suzerain. From this time, until the fall of Jerusalem, Judah alternated between nominal submission to Nebuchadnezzar and open revolt against him; but with few and brief exceptions the government was in the hands of the Egyptian party, who looked to the Pharaohs for help against Babylon. This party, to which the bulk of the nation adhered, was possessed by a great patriotic and religious enthusiasm. They were supported by the priests of the Temple, and by the guilds of professional prophets, in their reliance upon the ancient faith that Jehovah would deliver His chosen people. Each revolt was a Holy War. In spite of the deportation of Jehoiachin and the bulk of the ruling classes to Babylon, the remaining Jews maintained their enthusiasm and adhered to the same national policy.

v. The Prophet as Traitor and Heretic.—Individualism. Jeremiah's attitude during this period is accurately defined in Jehovah's words to him in i. 18: "I have made thee this day a defenced city, and an iron pillar, and brasen walls against the whole land, against the kings, princes, priests, and people of Judah. They shall fight against thee: but they shall not prevail against thee, for I am with thee to deliver thee—it is the utterance of Jehovah." Jeremiah stood almost alone in his opposition to the patriotic enthusiasm of the people, his attitude was not merely indifferent, but hostile, or—as it would seem to the ruling party—traitorous. He was continually urging submission to Babylon, the national enemy, the oppressor of Jehovah's people. In the last siege he urged individuals to desert to the enemy, and even tried to prevail on the king to surrender the city. And as the religion of the nation was for the moment merged in its patriotism, Jeremiah's teaching seemed abominable blasphemy, or, as we should say, rank heresy. One of his supporters was put to death, and he himself, on several occasions narrowly escaped a similar fate. Though Jeremiah in his teaching still emphasises the national character of Jewish religion, yet his attitude of defiant isolation implicitly asserts the main principles of individualism in religion. In virtue of his personal relation to Jehovah — his individual inspiration — Jeremiah claimed that his teaching was valid in the teeth of ancient usage and tradition, and in spite of the opposition of the nation and its constituted authorities, civil and religious. In other words, Jeremiah asserted the authority of the inspired individual as against formulated doctrine in Church and State, as against a National Government and a National Clergy. This is, doubtless, the attitude of all the prophets; but it is most manifest in Jeremiah.

vi. THE INEVITABLE RUIN OF JUDAH.—The situation of Judah was now closely parallel to that of Samaria under its last kings, and what Hosea was to Samaria, Jeremiah was to Judah. Jeremiah was conscious of this fact, and carefully studied the writings of Hosea, many of whose ideas and phrases he adopts and develops. While, as we have already seen, Jeremiah asserts Jehovah's willingness to forgive, he is none the less convinced that the ruin of Judah is inevitable, because the people are incapable of true repentance. They were a nation that did not "hearken to the voice of Jehovah their God, nor receive correction" (Jer. vii. 28). Sin had become a second nature to them. "Can the Ethiopian change his skin, or the leopard his spots? then may ye also do good, that are accustomed to do evil" (xiii. 23). Elsewhere (xv. 4), the ruin of Judah is spoken of as the punishment of the sin of Manasseh, as if subsequent repentance and amendment were in vain because Manasseh's sin was not yet expiated; but Jeremiah does not formulate this position, on the contrary he offers pardon to Jerusalem if a single righteous man can be found in her (v. 1). Although Jeremiah does not formally reconcile such passages as v. 1, and xv. 4, yet they are easily seen to be consistent. The sin of Manasseh ruins Judah, because Judah is possessed by it as by an evil spirit, persists in following in Manasseh's footsteps, and has no inclination to repent.

vii. THE REMNANT.—Jeremiah seems to have contemplated the entire destruction of the existing Jewish community: nevertheless, Israel was not to become extinct. According to iii. 12, Israel—*i.e.*, the Ten Tribes—is to return and take the place of Judah. After the deportation of Jehoiachin and his companions, Jeremiah saw the promise of the New Israel in the exiles at Babylon (xxiv. 4-7).

viii. THE JUDGMENT OF THE NATIONS.—Jeremiah saw in Nebuchadnezzar and the Chaldeans Jehovah's instrument for the chastisement of Judah (xxi. 4-7, xxv. 9),* but not of Judah only, but of all nations (ix. 25, 26, xxv. 15-33 †; cf. xlvi.-xlix.,) the latter having also been guilty of heinous sin (xxv. 31). Obviously the Chaldeans could not be included in a judgment which they themselves inflicted; but it is noteworthy that (with the doubtful exception of l., li.), Jeremiah neither declares the guilt of the Chaldeans, nor predicts their ruin.‡

ix. HABAKKUK, cir. B.C. 605.—On the other hand the "burden" of Habakkuk is Jehovah's vengeance on the Chaldeans (i. 12). This judgment rests on moral grounds, the Chaldeans are punished for their cruelty and injustice (ii. 9-17), and for their idolatry (ii. 18-20). Their ruin involves the restoration of all their victims as well as of the Jews: "Because thou hast spoiled many nations, all the remnant of the peoples shall spoil thee" (ii. 8). Habakkuk, like Nahum, stands apart from the main current of prophetic teaching: he neither emphasises the sin

---

* LXX. omits the clause "and Nebuchadnezzar, king of Babylon, my servant."

† LXX. omits the clause "and the king of Sheshach—*i.e.*, Babylon—shall drink after them."

‡ The text of xxv. 12-14 is probably corrupt.

nor announces the ruin of Judah. The Jews are "more righteous" than the "wicked" Chaldeans (i. 13): they are "the just who shall live by faith" (ii. 4). Moreover the words of ii. 20, "Jehovah is in His holy Temple: let all the earth keep silence before Him," would inevitably be used by Jeremiah's opponents to support their teaching that the inviolability of the Temple guaranteed the safety of Jerusalem.

x. EZEKIEL AND THE PALESTINIAN JEWS, cir. B.C. 592 -586.—Ezekiel was a priest who had been carried captive to Babylon with Jehoiachin in B.C. 599. In many respects his teaching is dependent upon that of Jeremiah, whose disciple and adherent he probably was before he went into exile. Like Jeremiah, he declares that all classes in Judah were sunk in moral, social and religious corruption (vii. 23, viii., xiii., xvi., xx., xxii., etc.); he denounces the alliance with Egypt (xvii. 15); he regards Nebuchadnezzar and the Chaldeans as the instruments chosen by Jehovah to execute His judgments upon Judah (xvii. 20, xxi. 8-24) and the nations (xxv.-xxxii.). Chaldea, moreover, is still exempted from any express condemnation. The bulk of the Jewish population will be exterminated and the "Remnant" carried into captivity (vi. 1-14). According to xvii. 11-21, the immediate occasion of the ruin of Judah was Zedekiah's treachery, in breaking the oath of allegiance which he had sworn to Nebuchadnezzar.

xi. THE FALL OF JERUSALEM, cir. B.C. 586.—The long series of prophecies of doom, which culminated in the utterances of Jeremiah, was now fulfilled by the final capture of Jerusalem, the destruction of the Holy City and the Temple, the massacre of many of the population, and the deportation of many more to Babylon. This catastrophe enforced afresh the lessons which had been taught by the Fall of Samaria. The captivity of the Ten Tribes had shown that Jehovah was not necessarily the champion of Israel, that His protection depended upon the conduct and character of His people, and that, if His chosen people gave themselves up to wickedness, they would be blotted out.

The effect of the fall of Samaria had been almost destroyed by the deliverance from Sennacherib, which, together with Isaiah's teaching, was construed into an unconditional guarantee that Jehovah would always protect Jerusalem and the Temple. This revival of ancient doctrine was again utterly discredited by the fall of Jerusalem. At the same time, the authority of Jeremiah, which had been shaken by the defeat and death of Josiah, was fully established by the exact fulfilment of his awful threats of ruin. The results of this terrible authentication of Jeremiah's teaching were instant and manifold. We may mention two important points:

(*a*) Revealed Religion survived Judah, as it had survived Israel, § 4, viii. Popular Jewish theology had sought to stake the honour, the very existence, of Jehovah, on the existence of Jerusalem and the Temple; but for the inspired protests of Jeremiah, the higher faith of Judah would have perished with Solomon's shrine. Jeremiah and Ezekiel had proclaimed that Nebuchadnezzar destroyed the Temple, not in spite of, but at the command of, Jehovah. As formerly at the fall of Samaria, so now the destruction of the chosen people testified to the omnipotence, instead of the impotence, of Jehovah. Moreover, it was clearly shown that Jehovah not only continued to exist, but that His majesty was unimpaired when His chosen people were slain or captive, His land a desolate and conquered province of a foreign empire, and His City and Temple a heap of ruins. Clearly, therefore, Jehovah was altogether independent of Israel. Thus another great step had been taken in the revelation of the omnipotence of Jehovah, and the universality of the true religion.

(b) The chastisement of Judah for its sin emphasised afresh the moral character of Jehovah, and the moral conditions of acceptance with Him.

xii. THE JEWISH REFUGEES IN EGYPT (Jer. xl.-xliv.).—The Fall of Jerusalem suggested the possibility that the long-threatened punishment had been fully inflicted, and that the Jews still left in Palestine might forthwith become the true Israel, reconciled to Jehovah and enjoying His favour. These hopes were promptly quenched by Ezekiel (xxxiii. 21-29). Moreover, the murder of the Chaldean governor, the Jewish prince Gedaliah, was followed by the flight of many of the remaining Jews into Egypt. Jeremiah had protested against this return to Egypt, in which he himself was compelled to join. The devotion of the Jews—especially the Jewish women—to the "Queen of Heaven" led to renewed threats of punishment in Jeremiah's last recorded prophecy.

In view of the intimate relations between Egypt and its Jewish partisans, large numbers of Jews must already have taken refuge in Egypt. These, with the new arrivals, formed the nucleus of the Jewish community in Egypt, which exercised so important an influence on the future of Judaism.

xiii. OBADIAH, cir. B.C. 586.—The cruelty of Edom towards the Jews, about the time of the capture of Jerusalem, drew down upon it the condemnation of the prophets, which finds special expression in a prophecy which occurs in two slightly different forms, as the Book of Obadiah and as Jer. xlix. 7-22. The subsequent conquest of Southern Judæa by the Edomites intensified the Jewish hatred of Edom (Joel iii. 19).

7. The Captivity. i. RELIGION A SPIRITUAL LIFE, AND NOT A RITUAL OBSERVANCE.—The prophetic teaching that the destruction of Jerusalem, the desolation of Palestine, and the exile of the Jews were the work of Jehovah involved (§ 6, xi.) a belief in Jehovah's independence of land and people, sanctuary and ritual. The experience of the Captivity confirmed this faith. In a foreign land, without Temple or sacrifice, the Jews still enjoyed the sense of Jehovah's presence and protection, and the ministry of prophets such as Ezekiel and the author of Isa. xl.-lxvi. If Jehovah was thus present in a hostile and alien country, He must be omnipresent. Moreover, the fact that the religious life of the faithful continued without sanctuary, sacrifice, or ritual, while their national life was in abeyance, was a revelation of the spiritual character of religion, and of its significance for the individual apart from the nation.

ii. LITERARY ACTIVITY.—The Jews in Babylon confidently expected to return to Palestine and renew their old national life. Hence they were anxious to retain all extant knowledge of that life, so that the Captivity was a period of great literary activity. In addition to original productions, of which we shall speak later on, older documents were combined and re-edited. The interruption of local tradition by the exile gave new importance to written history; and, at the same time, the teaching of the prophets had emphasised the religious significance of history. During the Captivity the ancient historical documents were combined and edited under the influence of Deuteronomy and the prophets. The ancient narratives of the Patriarchs, the Exodus, and the Conquest,* were combined with an enlarged edition of Josiah's Deuteronomy and Judges; Samuel and Kings were re-edited as a single, continuous, historical work. Probably the Book of Jeremiah was edited during this period in a form substantially the same as that in which it is now extant.

iii. THE FORMATION OF RITUAL CODES. — Deuteronomy lays comparatively little stress on the details of ritual. These would natually be a matter of hereditary tradition in the priestly families, though, of course, the tradition might be committed to writing. But the prolonged cessation of the Temple services during the Captivity might have led to the loss or corruption of a purely oral tradition. Hence it was necessary that ancient customs should be recorded in writing. Moreover, as these ancient customs had

* J. and E.

been tainted by many corruptions, the formation of written codes was an obvious opportunity for purging the ritual of impure elements, and of adapting it to the prophetic ideal of worship. This is attempted in two closely allied documents—the ritual code in Ezek. xl.-xlviii., and the Law of Holiness (Lev. xvii.-xxvi.).

iv. EZEKIEL XL.-XLVIII. —These chapters contain an ecclesiastical constitution and ritual code for the redeemed and purified Israel. The limitation of worship to a single sanctuary is confirmed (xliii.), and the supreme importance of the Temple is shown by minute architectural specifications and numerous other details occupying chapters xl.-xlii. As regards the priesthood, the revolution which began with the suppression of the high places is carried a stage further. Deuteronomy had given to all the priests of the high places the right to be included in the priesthood of the Temple; Josiah, however, had only been able to secure that they might be maintained out of the Temple revenues, they were not allowed to perform the priestly ministrations. Ezek. xliv. 9-16 entirely excludes the Levitical priests of the high places from the priesthood proper and reduces them—under the title of "the Levites"—to be menial servants of the priests. This degradation is the penalty inflicted upon them for their share in the corruptions of the high places. The priesthood proper is reserved for the hereditary priests of the Temple, the Levitical priests of the house of Zadok. Ezekiel carefully and exhaustively systematises the religious constitution of Israel. Order and decorum are to characterise the new dispensation; the inter-tribal and other divisions of his new map of Palestine are all straight lines; and the ground plan and elevations of the Temple are, as far as possible, square or symmetrical. The persons and institutions of the new Israel are sacred (*qadosh*, § 17) in a carefully ordered gradation.

v. THE LAW OF HOLINESS (LEV. XVII.-XXVI.).— This code, as the name now given to it implies, emphasises Ezekiel's principle of the sanctity (EV, holiness) of Israel. In other respects also the two codes have much in common. There is obviously a literary connection between them, some dependence of one upon the other, or of both upon previous documents; but the exact nature of the connection has not yet been determined. The law of holiness as we now have it contains editorial additions later than the exile.

The keynote of the law of holiness is struck by the command of Jehovah to Israel: "Ye shall be *qadosh* (E.V. "holy"); for I, Jehovah your God, am *qadosh*" (xix. 2. Cf., xx. 26). While this code strongly insists on moral and social righteousness (xviii.-xx., xxiv.) and further develops the humane tendencies of Deuteronomy and the prophets (xxv.); the sanctity of the people is specially connected with their abstinence from unclean food (xx. 25, 26), and the sanctity of the priests with similar external observances. It is taken for granted that the priests are not the Levites generally, but the "sons of Aaron"— *i.e.*, the house of Zadok. But the gradation of the Temple hierarchy is further developed and completed by the formal recognition of a single supreme head of the priesthood—the High Priest (xxi. 10-15). The limitation of sacrifice to a single sanctuary is again affirmed (xvii. 1-7). While in Ezek. xl.-xlviii. the stress is laid on the sacred land and the Temple, in the law of holiness the stress is laid on the sacred ritual, especially on ritual "cleanliness." While Ezekiel's scheme is a systematic reconstruction of ancient custom and tradition, the law of holiness is compiled and edited from earlier codes.

While Ezekiel and the law of holiness show no falling off from the ancient prophetic zeal for moral righteousness, their interest in ritual is in marked contrast to the attitude of Jeremiah, of the earlier prophets, and even of Deuteronomy. With the suppression of the high places and the purification of the Temple worship, the ritual ceased to be objectionable in itself. The combination of moral and ritual ordinances in the same documents was intended to secure that Israel should not again hope to find in its ritual impunity for an immoral life. At the same time the greater stress laid on ritual tempted the people to indulge the universal tendency to ignore the moral and spiritual life, in reliance upon external forms. It is significant that amongst the sins which led to the ruin of Judah, the one which the law of holiness selects for special mention is the non-observance of the sabbatical year (xxvi. 34-43).

vi. LAMENTATIONS.—This book is a retrospect which corresponds very closely to the prophecies of Jeremiah, who has often been supposed to be its author. It confesses that the misery of the Jews is inflicted by Jehovah as the just punishment of sin (i. 18), especially the sin of the priests and prophets (ii. 14, iv. 13).

vii. ISAIAH XL.-LXVI.—We have already seen how the fall of Jerusalem and the Captivity emphasised the universality of religion and the omnipotence and omnipresence of Jehovah. The situation of believing Jews in Chaldea compelled them to reflect on these questions. They might believe that the ruin of Judah was a manifestation of the power and righteousness of Jehovah, but the heathen were convinced that the chosen people had suffered through the impotence of Jehovah, and the might of heathen deities; and this conviction was shared by many of the Jews themselves (Jer. xliv. 18, 19). Moreover, the captives in Babylon could not fail to be impressed by the magnificent temples and splendid ritual of the Chaldean religion. They would be tempted to regard the extent and prosperity of the empire as another proof of the power of its gods.

Ezekiel was specially anxious to vindicate the name of Jehovah from the reproach which the heathen cast upon it, on account of the sufferings of Judah. The presence of the captives amongst the heathen brought dishonour on Jehovah (xxxvi. 16-24), so that, by a series of judgments (xxv.-xxxii.) they must be taught to know " that I am Jehovah " (xxv. 7 *et passim*).

In Isa. xl.-lxvi. the controversy between Jehovah and the gods of Babylon is decided by a formal, explicit, and, in part, reasoned statement of the exclusive deity of Jehovah (xliv. 6, xlv. 5); His omnipotence (xl.), and omniscience (xlviii. 1-8); He has created the world (xl. 28, xlv. 12) and governs it by His Providence (xliv. 7). On the other hand the gods of Babylon are as helpless and useless as the idols by which they are represented (xli. 23, 24, xliv. 9-20, xlvi. 1, 2). But Jehovah offers Himself as a Saviour to all mankind (xlv. 23-24), and commissions His servant Israel to be "a light to the Gentiles," and His "salvation unto the end of the earth" (xlix. 6). The contrast between this high mission and the present degraded and wretched lot of even righteous exiles, showed that suffering was not always the punishment of sin; and Isa. liii. explains the sufferings of the Righteous One as a vicarious atonement for the guilty.

viii. THE PROMISE OF RESTORATION.—We have seen that almost all the prophets couple with their prophecies of ruin, a promise of restoration. In the prophets of the close of the monarchy, the prophecies of a captivity are combined with a promise of return from captivity. According to Jer. xxv. 11, the captivity was to terminate after seventy years, and in xxx.-xxxiii.* the restoration of Israel and Judah is set forth at great length. Ezekiel regards the return of Israel and Judah as necessary to the vindication of the honour of Jehovah (xxix. 21, xxxvi. 9—38, xxxvii.); and although Isa. xl.-lxvi. declares that Jehovah is the God of all mankind, these chapters, nevertheless, assert that Jehovah has chosen Israel to be His servant (xliv. 1), through whom He is revealed to the world. Accordingly

* Even if the Jeremianic authorship of these chapters in their present form be disputed, the main idea of the restoration of Israel and Judah is certainly Jeremiah's.

ISRAEL IN HISTORY

the Jews are to be restored to Judah (xl. etc.). According to Ezek. xxxvi. 22, Israel is restored not for its own sake, but simply to vindicate Jehovah's honour. Like the Exodus, the conquest and the deliverance from Sennacherib, the restoration is a free act of divine sovereignty; a fresh token of the divine election of Israel, which is not brought about through any merit on the part of the chosen people. Similarly Isa. xl.-lxvi. emphasises the election of Israel; but this renewal of divine favour is rendered possible, because by the sufferings of the Captivity, the Jews had expiated the former sins of the nation: " Speak ye comfortably to Jerusalem, and cry unto her that her warfare is accomplished, that her iniquity is pardoned; that she hath received of Jehovah's hand double for all her sins " (xl. 2). The same idea underlies Jer. xxx.—xxxiii. (Cf. li. 20.*)

Meanwhile, the comparatively favourable attitude of Jeremiah and Ezekiel towards Babylon is changed for one of stern condemnation. Like Assyria, Babylon has been the instrument which Jehovah had chosen to chastise His people; but also, like Assyria, Babylon had not recognised its subordinate position. The Chaldeans had become lifted up with pride, had blasphemed Jehovah, and had gone beyond their commission; and had treated the Jews with undue harshness and cruelty (xlvii. 6). Hence Jer. l.* li.* and Isaiah xlvii., xiii.,* xiv.,* follow Habakkuk in announcing the speedy ruin of Chaldea as the punishment of its sins.

* The authenticity of these chapters is denied by many authorities.

As previous prophets had indicated Assyria and Babylon as the instruments of Jehovah's judgments, and Jeremiah and Ezekiel had given special prominence to Nebuchadnezzar as the sword and servant of Jehovah, so now Isaiah (xliv. 28, xlvi.) declares that Cyrus, king of Persia, is Jehovah's shepherd and Messiah (E.V. "Anointed"), who shall execute judgment upon Babylon and deliver the Jews.

ix. THE FALL OF BABYLON AND THE RETURN OF THE JEWS, B.C. 538-6.—Thus the conquests of Cyrus, and especially his occupation of Babylon, and the subsequent return of a portion of the Jews to Palestine furnished new proofs of the lordship of Jehovah over the nations, and of the authority of the prophets. One feature of the new deliverance of Israel exercised considerable influence upon the future of Judaism. While at the Conquest and under the judges and the earlier kings Jehovah delivered Israel through its own victorious armies, the termination of the Captivity, like the Exodus and the deliverance from Sennacherib, was brought about without any aid from the Jews themselves. The former deliverances had shown that Jehovah controlled Nature in the interests of Israel; the Return proved that the history of the nations was similarly governed. The Jews found their condition as a subject-race less intolerable, when they believed that the fortunes of their rulers, and indeed the international relations of all the known world, were divinely ruled in their interests.

8. Judaism. i. THE RESTORED COMMUNITY AND THE JEWISH DISPERSION.—By the return of a number of Jews from Babylon to Judæa, and their re-union with some, at any rate, of the remnant who had continued in their native land throughout the Captivity, the chosen people were once more represented by a Jewish community in the sacred land. But this community was no longer independent; it inhabited a subdivision of a province—one might almost say a city—of the Persian empire. It was for some time, and always to a large extent, a city-state. Its *raison-d'être* was the maintenance of the Temple and its services; so that, as it is often said, Israel was no longer a nation; it had become a church.

At the same time the Jews who remained behind in Babylon formed a much more powerful and important body than the little colony round Jerusalem; and, although in one sense the Jewish community in Egypt dates from the foundation of Alexandria, yet, as we have seen, there was already a body of Jewish refugees in Egypt who prepared the way for the Alexandrian settlement. Henceforward, therefore, Judaism had three centres, Egypt, Judæa, and Babylon; and the Jewish dispersion becomes an important factor in the development of Judaism.

ii. THE REBUILDING OF THE TEMPLE, B.C. 536-516; HAGGAI, B.C. 520; ZECHARIAH i.-viii., B.C. 520-518.—The first task of the returned exiles was the restoration of the sacrificial ritual and the rebuilding of the Temple (Ezra iii.-vi.). The zeal of the new community for purity of worship is shown by their refusal to unite with the mixed population of Samaria (Ezra iv. 1-4). After many delays, and in the teeth of much opposition, the Temple was completed and dedicated. Thus the special interest of Jehovah in the chosen people and the sacred land was again set forth in the visible symbols of a sacred building and ritual. The one Temple accepted by all acknowledged Jews as the only sanctuary of Jehovah became a visible token of the divine unity; while in the absence of the ark (Jer. iii. 16), or any other visible symbol of the divine presence, the very emptiness of the Most Sacred Place emphasised the spirituality of the divine nature.

The Jews were encouraged to rebuild the Temple by the exhortations of Haggai and Zechariah, who promised that Jehovah would bless the work and reward the zeal of the Jews by great prosperity.

iii. THE REFORMS OF EZRA AND NEHEMIAH, cir. B.C. 458-433; THE LEVITICAL LAW (Priestly Code, P.), MALACHI.—The Temple and its ritual did not, however, prove a sufficient safeguard of pure religion. The small Jewish community was surrounded by kindred tribes, including the semi-Israelite population of Samaria. These had been excluded from any share in the rebuilding of the Temple; but the Jews necessarily had some dealings with their neighbours, and, as after a while this intercourse increased, many—even among the rulers and priests—married foreign wives (Ezra ix. 1-4), and at one time an Ammonite, Tobiah (Neh. xiii. 4-9), * was allowed to occupy a store-chamber of the Temple. Proper provision was not made for the services (Neh. xiii. 10),

* The events of Neh. xiii. happened after the main reformation, but they may serve as mild examples of the previous state of affairs.

The same causes were at work which had corrupted the life and worship of ancient Israel, and it seemed probable that the good effect of the teaching of the prophets and the discipline of the Captivity would be lost. The loyalty of the Jews to the new order was tried by great distress, during which the more wealthy made great profits out of the necessities of the poor (Neh. v.). The Sabbath was almost altogether neglected (Neh. xiii.).

The Jewish community was delivered from these dangers, and finally won for pure religion by the persistent efforts of Ezra and Nehemiah. They largely succeeded in effecting that complete separation between the Jews and their neighbours, which Joshua and Zerubbabel had attempted to bring about. Nehemiah provided for the continued existence of the Jews as a separate community, by fortifying Jerusalem. Jews who had married foreigners were compelled to put away their wives, and such marriages were strictly forbidden (Ezra ix., x.; Neh. xiii. 23-28). Measures were taken to relieve the distress amongst the people (Neh. v.), and to secure the maintenance of the Temple services (Neh. x., xiii. 10-14, 29-31).

The great instrument which Ezra and Nehemiah used in effecting their reforms was the Levitical law. This document, which is extant in Leviticus and the allied portions of the rest of the Pentateuch, and of Joshua, contains an elaborate system of public and private ritual on the lines of Ezek. xl.-xlviii., and the law of holiness. The latter was soon included in the Levitical law. The principles of this new code were very similar to those of its predecessors; it presents the same combination of moral and ritual ordinances, but even when the law of holiness is reckoned as part of the Levitical law, the stress laid upon ritual far outweighs all other interests. This new code is combined with a brief introductory history of the ancestors of Israel, and of the Exodus. Here the teaching of the prophets is illustrated in narrative form; an account is given of the creation of the universe by God; His eternal and almighty Providence is shown, shaping all history towards the establishment of the Israelite Kingdom of God in Palestine; His election of Israel is set forth as the climax of a series of elections; His method of progressive revelation is seen in the successive revelations by which He was known to the first patriarchs as Elohim, to Abraham as El-shaddai, to Moses as Jehovah.

Ezekiel's systematisation of the ritual is here extended to an almost mathematical gradation of sacred things. Only at a single supremely sacred point of ritual does Israel fully realise its communion with Jehovah. Thus the exaltation of the divine majesty is strikingly emphasised, but, at the same time, the system shows a marked advance towards the transcendental monotheism of later Judaism. It is noteworthy that this supreme act of communion, the entry of the High Priest into the Most Sacred Place on the Day of Atonement, is connected with the expiation of sin. Here again we have the permanent expression in ritual of the prophetic teaching as to the corruption of Judah and the constant need of divine forgiveness.

Thus the intimate, direct and joyous fellowship of ancient Israel with its God was replaced by a worship mediated through a ritual and a priesthood, and pervaded with a humiliating and depressing sense of sin and of the need of atonement.

As, under Josiah, Deuteronomy had been accepted by a solemn covenant as the national code of morality and worship, and thus received the rank of canonical scripture; so now the Levitical law, either by itself or in combination with the rest of the Pentateuch, was accepted by a second and equally solemn covenant as the divine standard of life and worship, and became the Jewish Scriptures (Neh. viii.).

The Book of Malachi is linked with the reforms of Ezra and Nehemiah. Amongst the sins it denounces are niggardliness in offering sacrifices (i. 7-14), withholding the payment of priestly dues (iii. 8-10), " dealing treacherously with the wife of his youth " (ii. 14-16)—*i.e.*, possibly putting her away in order to take a foreign wife.

Many Psalms also express intense enthusiasm for the law, the priesthood, and the ritual (xix., cxviii., cxix., etc.).

iv. THE SAMARITANS.—One result of the successful exclusion of the semi-Israelites of Samaria from the Jewish community was the formation of a second community of worshippers of Jehovah—the Samaritans. These last accepted the Pentateuch as canonical in a special text of their own, and erected on Mt. Gerizim a second Temple to Jehovah. Josephus (Antt. xi., vii. 2, and viii. 2, 4) places the building of this temple in the time of Alexander the Great; but the Samaritan community probably dates from Nehemiah's expulsion from Jerusalem of that grandson of Eliashib the High Priest, who was son-in-law of Sanballat the Horonite (Neh. xiii. 28).

v. ANTI-LEGAL TENDENCIES WITHIN JUDAISM. RUTH (?); JONAH (?); PROVERBS; JOB; ECCLESIASTES; PSALMS.—The exceptional prominence given to ritual by the Levitical law and later Judaism is by no means an accurate representation of the spiritual tendencies of the period between the Return and the Maccabees. Ezra carried through his reforms in the teeth of the opposition of the ruling classes, civil and ecclesiastical, and largely relied on the authority of the Persian suzerain. The literature of the period shows that many earnest Jews were comparatively indifferent to ritual, and preoccupied with the more directly spiritual side of religion. If the Book of Ruth is correctly referred to this period, its sympathetic treatment of marriages between Israelites and Moabites is in marked contrast to the attitude of Ezra and Nehemiah. The Book of Jonah censures the prophet for his lack of sympathy with a Gentile city, and depicts the repentance of Nineveh as accepted by Jehovah. Psalms like li. 16, 17 anxiously deprecate any undue faith in ritual. The wisdom literature—Job, Proverbs, Ecclesiastes, and the Psalter—generally display very little interest in legal ordinances. We have moreover to remember that throughout this period the great prophets were carefully studied and edited, so that their influence was continually felt in support of moral and spiritual religion.

vi. DIVINE JUSTICE AND THE SUFFERINGS OF THE

RIGHTEOUS (cf. § 31); JOB; ECCLESIASTES.—We have already seen how large a part the doctrine of the close relation of sin and suffering played in the controversies between the prophets and the Jews; and how such events as the death of Josiah, rendered the current teaching a continual stumbling block to Jewish faith. The circumstances of the restored community raised this question with renewed intensity, both for the community and the individual. The Jews were consciously righteous as they had never been before, they were carefully observing the divine law; and if their obedience to God was more exact in external observances than in moral and spiritual life, they had no Isaiah or Jeremiah to force that fact on their attention. Indeed, whatever their faults may have been, within their own community the Jews probably attained a high level of brotherhood and social righteousness. Yet they were the subjects of a foreign power, and often suffered outrage from hostile neighbours or oppression from their masters; they still experienced unfavourable seasons, and had to contend with all the difficulties which beset a small state in a poor country. The question of Habakkuk (i. 13), "Wherefore lookest thou upon them that deal treacherously, and holdest thy peace when the wicked swalloweth up the man that is more righteous than he?" was constantly upon men's lips; it is the theme of many Psalms—*e.g.*, iii., vii., x., xvii., xxii., xxxv., xxxvii., etc., etc. At the same time men's attitudes towards this question varied according to the circumstances of their time and their personal fortunes. The question became acute when evil days fell upon Judah, or when a righteous man was overwhelmed by oppression; in prosperous times wealthy Jews were willing to follow the ancient doctrine, and interpret their prosperity as a sign of divine favour without considering how this doctrine bore on the sufferers of less fortunate times; indeed, they were often content to believe that the latter suffered on account of their many sins. These alternations of feeling are reflected in the documents of the period. There is no evidence that the teaching of Isa. liii. (vii. § 7), made much immediate impression, though we know that the doctrine of vicarious atonement exercised great influence on Pharisaic Judaism, and became a fundamental doctrine of Christianity. Before such teaching could be fully accepted, men had to reconsider and, indeed, reconstruct the current doctrine of the relation of sin and suffering; and it was difficult to overthrow a view which necessarily commended itself to all prosperous and successful persons. While the main section of the Book of Job is a passionate polemic against this doctrine, the Elihu speeches are a later addition intended to refute the error of this polemic, and to justify the ancient creed. Similarly the view of history given in the Book of Chronicles is intended to illustrate and establish the same doctrine. On the other hand, Ecclesiastes cuts away the foundations of the old faith by maintaining that the material prosperity, which was supposed to be a token of divine favour and acceptance, was itself empty and worthless, "vanity of vanities," "vanity and vexation of spirit" (R.V. "striving after wind,' Marg. "feeding on wind"). This negation prepared the way for the recognition of spiritual blessedness as the highest good, a position which is suggested, rather than explicitly asserted, by isolated passages in the Psalms and elsewhere (xvii. 15).

vii. INDIVIDUALISM (cf. ch. vi.).—Even a national religion necessarily has an individualistic aspect; the religious consciousness of the citizen is never wholly merged in that of the community, he is always conscious that the national religion has some personal interest and value for himself. And although the prophets dealt almost exclusively with the relations of Jehovah and Israel, yet the conditions under which they taught compelled them to emphasise indirectly this individualistic side of religion. Under normal conditions an Israelite's religion was determined by his nationality; it was no question of personal choice.

The prophets, however, were mostly in an attitude of antagonism to the nation generally, and to the popular customs and traditions of its faith. They sought to convert the people to their teaching, and claimed that their followers constituted the true Israel of God. Thus, for the adherents of the prophets, religious faith and practice had ceased to be determined by national status, and had become a matter of personal choice, which almost always separated the believer from the bulk of his fellow-countrymen, and sometimes placed him in opposition to what was generally regarded as the national religion. See specially the case of Jeremiah.

After the return, pure Jehovah-worship became finally established as the Jewish faith, though a large minority seems always to have been indifferent or hostile to the law; loyalty to which was still rather an individual choice than absolute matter of course. Moreover, the personal ritual of the Levitical law, the regulations as to cleanness and the elaborate ceremonial connected with everyday life, were too numerous and complicated to be observed merely as habits, the law could only be kept by deliberate and zealous personal effort. Then, too, the circumstances of the dispersion gave prominence to the individual religious life. Jewish families and clans were often isolated among the Gentiles. Their faith was sustained by pride of race, by their confidence in the exclusive religious privileges of Israel. But thus, even their national faith became a personal matter. The ancient Israelite held his national faith as a member of a visible community gathered in their own land; but the national faith separated the Jew of the dispersion from his Gentile neighbours, and became almost an individual privilege, a personal distinction. And again, the problem of the sufferings of the righteous became more and more a question of personal religion, not only because it was naturally illustrated by personal experience and most keenly felt in individual cases, but also because, in the scattered condition of the Jews, they no longer shared a common national life, and it was impossible to discuss the problem from the point of view of the nation as a whole.

We have also illustrated these facts from the stress laid by the Levitical law on private ritual, and from the discussions of the problems of personal suffering in the prophets, Psalms, Job, and Ecclesiastes. Another illustration of the individualistic tendency is found in Proverbs, which is almost exclusively occupied with individual conduct. Moreover, in the post-exile period the Psalms seem to have circulated widely in larger or smaller collections. Many are liturgical, and in many others the author spoke originally in the name of the community. But the experience of centuries shows how readily most of the Psalms adapt themselves to the spiritual needs of the individual. The demand for these written Psalters arose from this adaptability to individual needs, and the use of such Psalters tended to foster and develop individual religion.

viii. THE ANTAGONISM OF JUDAISM AND THE GENTILE WORLD. THE BOOK OF ESTHER.—The exclusive claims which the Jews made for Jehovah and for themselves necessarily cut them off from the fellowship of other nations, and created mutual dislike between themselves and the Gentiles. It was one thing to claim that Jehovah was absolute Lord of the fortunes of Israel, or even supreme among the gods; it was quite another to exhaust the resources of contemptuous sarcasm in showing that Bel and Nebo were mere senseless blocks of wood and stone, that no word of divine truth had reached mankind except through the Jews, and that the only path of salvation led beneath the yoke of submission to the civil and religious dominion of Israel. Contempt met contempt, and found expression as in the last days of Judæa, in mutual outrage. The Book of Esther and such Psalms as vii., xxxv., lxix., cix., are the monuments of this hostile relation between Jews and Gentiles. These documents, which justify the Jew as against the Gentiles, follow on the lines of Nahum and Habakkuk, rather than on those of the other prophets, who condemn Israelite and Gentile alike.

ix. THE PERSECUTIONS OF ANTIOCHUS EPIPHANES. THE BOOK OF DANIEL. THE MACCABEES, cir. B.C. 170-160.—At the same time the antagonism between Jew and Gentile was, as we have seen, accompanied by a division within the community of Judæa. The old predilection for foreign ideas and habits had by no means disappeared; and the Greek conquest of the East by Alexander the Great (B.C. 334-323) exposed the Jews to the almost irresistible fascinations of Hellenism. While the Temple priesthood accepted the privileges conferred upon them by the Levitical law, they seem to have had little zeal for Judaism as a religion, and to have left the maintenance and development of the law to the scribes, "the doctors of the law." Indeed, in the establishment of the Levitical law (in B.C. 444), Ezra, the scribe, and Nehemiah, the Persian governor, took the lead, and the priests are scarcely mentioned. Thus the priesthood offered no very enthusiastic opposition to the party who wished to leaven Judaism with Hellenistic ideas. The Jews were delivered from this new danger by the persecutions of Antiochus Epiphanes. The attempt to suppress their national ritual, and to destroy all copies of their Law, roused the patriotic spirit and religious enthusiasm of the Jews. The narratives of the Book of Daniel nerved the martyrs to endurance, and their hopes were kindled by its visions of the ruin of their oppressors. Consolation was found for the cruel deaths of martyrs, in the faith that they would awake to everlasting life and their persecutors to shame and everlasting contempt (Dan. xii. 2). Psalms xliv., lx., and lxxiv., are often referred to this period of persecution. The heroism and diplomacy of the Maccabees shook off the yoke of the Syrian kings, and won a brief independence for the Jews. As the Maccabees were priests, Psalms cxv. and cxviii. which sing the praises of the House of Aaron, have been supposed to celebrate their triumph, and the ruler who is "a priest for ever after the order of Melchizedek" (Psalm cx. 4) has sometimes been identified with some one of the Maccabæans, who were at once civil rulers, and held the high priesthood not by legitimate descent, but by special divine appointment.

CHAPTER III

THE IDEAL ISRAEL

CHAPTER III

THE IDEAL ISRAEL

9. The Kingdom. i. THE MESSIANIC PROPHECIES.
—The standards set before Israel in the legislative codes and in the prophetic teachings were alike ideal, inasmuch as neither of them was ever even approximately realised. But, at any rate, these supplied the ethical and ritual canons which practically guided the people; and the Jehovist leaders and teachers attempted, at various times, to make the national life conform to them—with some degree of success. In this limited sense, the law and the prophets may be said to give us a picture of the normal Israel.

But the prophets were inspired with an ultimate ideal for Israel, which was incapable of immediate application to actual circumstances—the ideal expressed by the Messianic prophecies. No exact line can be drawn between the two; Ezek. xl.-xlviii. is a curious blending of transcendental ideals with detailed legislation which served—and doubtless was intended to serve—as a practical basis for the life of the restored community. On the other hand the prophet's pictures of the ideal glory of Israel are constantly combined with predictions of more immediate application.

The distinction between the normal and the ideal Israel may be stated thus : the normal Israel was a standard to which the actual life of Israel was, in some measure, conformed : the ideal Israel involved a new dispensation in which the actual Israel was to be, not so much reformed, as transfigured. Moreover, reformations, which assimilated the life of Israel to the standard of the normal Israel, might be brought about by the nation itself and its human rulers ; but the changes which were to inaugurate the ideal Israel—the Messianic Kingdom of God— were to be brought about by the special intervention of Jehovah. Similarly, the prophecies concerning the ideal Israel differ from predictions, such as those of the deliverance from Sennacherib and the Return, inasmuch as the latter connect directly with Israel's actual circumstances, while the former postulate a new departure. At the same time the ideal Israel is always described in terms of the constitution and experiences of the actual Israel, and is thought of as arising out of the historical situation of the prophet's age.

We might say that approximately in the O. T. the Messianic Kingdom bears the same relation to the Levitical law, that in the N. T. the Second Coming and the Millennium bear to the Sermon on the Mount ; and as in the N. T. the Second Coming is almost always thought of as about to happen in the near future ; so to the prophets—the messengers of Him to whom a thousand years are as one day—the "Day of Jehovah" is always to-morrow. Hence their prophecies often have a double aspect—a limited application to the immediate future, and an ideal element which is to be realised in the Messianic Kingdom. The prophets themselves do not, as a rule, distinguish these two aspects.

ii. THE PREPARATION FOR THE KINGDOM.—All previous history, together with the historical situation of the prophet's own time, and its immediate sequel, are the preparation for the inauguration of the ideal Israel. This principle underlies the Deuteronomic interpretation of history; the history of the world from the creation, prefixed to the Levitical law; and the historical retrospects of Psalms lxxvii.-lxxix., cv.-cvii. Similarly, the prophets constantly appeal to history as illustrating the divine purpose which is to be ultimately realised in the true Israel; Isa. v. 2, xli., xliii., xliv. 1-8, etc.; Jer. xxx.-xxxiii.; Ezek. xxxix. 23-29.

This idea is most strikingly expressed in the Apocalyptic literature; *e.g.*, in Daniel we have a series of visions, which set forth the history of the East in the post-exilic period as leading up to the great deliverance from Antiochus.

iii. THE DAY OF JEHOVAH (E.V. " of the Lord ").— The epoch which is to inaugurate the new era is " The Day of Jehovah," or " that day " (so *passim* in all the prophets) in which, amid portents in the heavens, place will be made for the New Israel by the destruction of the old Israel (Samaria,—Amos, Hosea, Isaiah; Judah,—all the pre-exilic prophets except Nahum, Habakkuk, and perhaps Hosea), and of the heathen states and empires (all the prophets either generally or as to individual realms), a Remnant (cf § 6, vii.) will be preserved to be the seed of the new Israel.

The return of the exiles from Babylon and the establishment of a Jewish community which renounced idolatry and was faithful to the divine law, altered the form of prophetic teaching as to the Day of Jehovah. So far as "that day" involved the ruin of Israel and Judah, and even of the international system and great empires of the heathen world, it had been accomplished; and sanguine Jews indulged the hope that, both as to inner righteousness and external splendour, the restored community was to realise the glory of the New Israel. But the fulfilment of these hopes was deferred. Judaism remained outwardly weak and inwardly corrupt; and first Persia, and then the Greek kingdoms of Egypt and Syria took the place formerly filled by Assyria and Babylon. Hence, the Jews still looked forward to a Day of Jehovah, which should be a further judgment on the Gentiles, and at last inaugurate the long-deferred bliss of the new Israel. Even in Ezek. xxxviii., xxxix., Israel after its restoration to Palestine is assailed by Gog and the combined hosts of the enemies, and these perish miserably. Similarly, Micah v.,* Joel iii., Haggai ii. 6-9, 20-23; Zech. i, 21, xii., xiv., contemplate the overthrow of the heathen as a prelude to the complete and final restoration of Israel.* In Daniel, as in Ezekiel, the restoration is followed by new tribulation, the Prince Messiah, the Anointed Prince is cut

* Micah v., and Zech. xii., xiv., are often supposed to be pre-exilic.

off and the city and sanctuary are destroyed (ix. 25, 26). The final Day of Jehovah—the term, however, is not used here—is introduced by a time of unprecedented trouble, the final doom and deliverance are wrought by the archangel Michael, and are not so much a judgment of the nations and a deliverance of Israel, as a personal judgment of the righteous and wicked, preceded by a resurrection of the dead (xii.).

Similarly, the post-exilic literature renews in a different form the ancient teaching of the judgment upon Israel in the day of Jehovah. But the Jewish community is not definitely threatened, as Samaria and Judah had been, with ruin and captivity. The judgment is rather one of purification than of destruction. In Micah v. 10-14, horses and chariots, cities and fortresses, witchcraft and soothsayers and idols are to be cut off out of Israel; but also all its enemies are to be extirpated. In Joel grievous trouble is to come upon Israel in the Day of Jehovah, but this is to issue in deliverance and the abundant outpouring of the Divine Spirit. So in Zech. iii., iv., v., Israel is purged of its sin; and in Zech. xiii., Israel is purged of prophets and the spirit of uncleanness (2), two-thirds of the inhabitants are to be exterminated and the remainder spared (7-9). Similarly, in Malachi, the messenger of the covenant purifies the sons of Levi (iii. 1-3), and as in Dan. xii., so in Mal. iv., God destroys the wicked and saves the righteous.

iv. THE NEW ISRAEL.—The new Israel was to be constituted by the return and reunion of the two branches of the old Israel—Ephraim and Judah—as represented in each case by the Remnant. This is thought of in Hosea vi. 2 and Ezek. xxxvii. as the resurrection of the nation. Such is the unanimous teaching of the prophets who give the picture of the restoration in any detail (Isa. x. 20-23, xi. 10-16, xliii. 1-7; Jer. xxiii. 5-8, xxxi. 27-34; Ezek. xxxvii. 15-28). The establishment of the returned exiles at Jerusalem was never accepted as a complete fulfilment of these prophecies, even as far as Judah was concerned; the post-exilic prophets continued to expect the return of the dispersed Jews, as well as of the Ten Tribes, Zech. viii. 7-15; but after a time the Ten Tribes were forgotten, and Malachi, Joel, and Daniel seem conscious of no other Israel than the Jews of Judæa and the dispersion. Thus the ancient national and religious unity of Israel was restored, not by the reunion of the Ten Tribes with Judah, but by their final disappearance from Israel.

v. PALESTINE AS THE HOME OF THE NEW ISRAEL.—The sacred land was to be, as of old, the home of the chosen people, and was to be rendered more worthy of its high vocation by the transformation of its physical features. There was to be a great river full of fish flowing from the Temple to the Dead Sea, and the waters of the Dead Sea were to be healed (Ezek. xlvii. 1-12. Cf. Zech. xiv. 1-11). The land was to be endowed with extraordinary fertility (Isa. xxx. 23-26, xxxii. 15; Ezek. xxxiv. 26, 27, xlvii. 9-12; Joel ii. 18, iii. 18; Amos ii. 13; Zech. viii. 12; Mal. iii. 11, 12). The wild beasts were to become tame and harmless (Isa. xi. 1-9, lxv. 25). The Israelites would enjoy long life (lxv. 20-22) in this Paradise regained.

According to Ezek. xlviii., the new Israel was to content itself with occupying Palestine west of Jordan; but, according to Obad. 19, Benjamin was to inhabit Gilead.

vi. THE CONSTITUTION OF THE NEW ISRAEL.—The scheme in Ezek. xlviii. reproduces the main features of the life of ancient Israel—the division into two kingdoms of course excepted. The ancient tribes, the monarchy, the City of Jerusalem, the Temple and its priesthood were all to be revived; and the restoration of these institutions is for the most part taken for granted by all the prophets.

vii. MORAL AND SPIRITUAL PERFECTION.—The new Israel is to be perfect, freed both from moral corruption, and from false faith and worship. The people is to be wholly consecrated to Jehovah (Zech. xiv. 20, 21), and the soil is to be cultivated by foreign slaves, while the Israelites worship their God (Isa. lxi. 4-6).

viii. THE NEW COVENANT.—The constant backsliding and persistent impenitence of the old Israel had shown that Israel of itself was incapable of consistent loyalty to Jehovah. Therefore the ancient covenant which sought to discipline Israel by rewards and punishments is to be done away with. Jehovah will no longer rule by external constraint, but by the influence of His Spirit in the hearts of men. He no longer looks to chastisement to produce amendment, but will, Himself, change the nature of Israel and give it a new heart. The divine revelation is to be written on the heart rather than in books; men are to be independent of religious teachers. Each individual is to possess direct knowledge of Jehovah (Jer. xxxi. 31-34, xxxii. 39, 40; Ezek. xxxvi. 26, 27). Ezekiel, however, does not limit himself to the "new heart of flesh," and the "new spirit" which Jehovah is to implant in His people. He also conceives the new Israel as organised on the basis of a ritual and legislative code.

ix. ISRAEL AND THE HEATHEN.—Israel is to be free from foreign dominion, and to dwell securely in unbroken peace (Isa. liv. 17; Ezek. xxxiv. 28; Micah iv. 4). It is to be supreme over all other nations, and they are to minister to it with their labour and wealth (Isa. xlix. 22, 23, lx., lxi. 4-6; Hag. ii. 7, 8). Some passages even suggest that the new Israel will ultimately embrace all the nations of the earth—*e.g.*, in Isa. xix. 18-25, Egypt and Assyria are ranked with Israel as peoples of Jehovah.

x. RELIGIOUS SUPREMACY OF ISRAEL.—The Temple at Jerusalem is to become the great place of pilgrimage and worship for all mankind, the centre of revelation (Isa. ii. 1-4; Micah iv. 1-3; Isa. xlv. 14, lvi. 1-8, lx.; Zech. xiv. 16-19).

Israel, as the servant of Jehovah, is to teach His will to the Gentiles (Isa. xlii. 4-6, xlix. 6, lxvi. 19, 20).

xi. THE KINGDOM OF GOD.—Jehovah is the Divine King of the new Israel as of the old, and it is, therefore, the eternal Kingdom of God among men.

10. The Messiah. i. MESSIAH AS KING.—To speak of the Messiah as King would have been a truism to the ancient Israelite, because " Jehovah's Anointed," or "Messiah," was a familiar title of the Israelite kings (1 Sam. xvi. 6, etc.). Dan. ix. 25, 26, is the chief O. T. passage which has made " Messiah " a kind of technical term for the divinely sent Deliverer of Israel.*

The fact that the term Messiah could be so understood, and that afterwards it was universally and permanently adopted to denote this Deliverer, shows that He was chiefly thought of as the King of Israel.

In one sense Jehovah was, Himself, the King of Israel, but in the old Israel the Heavenly King had His earthly representative and counterpart, in the reigning sovereign of the house of David; and so in the new Kingdom of God the one conspicuous figure is the King, Jehovah's Anointed or Messiah, the Prince of the house of David.

Most of the prophets connect the future destiny of Israel with the house of David. The child of Isa. ix. 7 is to sit " upon the throne of David," and be over his kingdom, to establish and uphold it with judgment and righteousness from henceforth even for ever. In Isa. xi. 1, the deliverer is a rod out of the stem of Jesse. In Isa. xvi. 5, the king who is to reign " in truth . . . judging, and seeking judgment," is to have " his throne . . . established in mercy in the tent of David." Hosea iii. 5 looks

* Messiah even here is often interpreted of the succession of post-exilic high priests.

forward to the time when "the Israelites shall return and seek Jehovah their God, and David their king." Amos ix. 11 promises that the Lord "will raise up the tabernacle of David." In Micah v. 2, "the ruler in Israel" is to come forth from Bethlehem, David's birthplace. In Jer. xxiii. 5, 6, xxxiii. 15, 16, Jehovah raises up unto David a righteous branch (*çemaḥ*, growth. Cf. Isa. iv. 2), a wise and prudent King whose name is Jehovah *Çidqenu*—Jehovah is our righteousness. In Ezek. xxxiv. 23, 24, xxxvii. 24, 25, "My servant David" is to be the shepherd and prince of restored and reunited Israel. Zech. iii. 8 applies Jeremiah's prophecy of the "righteous branch" to Zerubbabel, the prince of the house of David, and in Hag. ii. 23 Zerubbabel is the chosen of Jehovah. In Zech. xii. 8 it is said that when "Jehovah defends the inhabitants of Jerusalem" "the house of David shall be as God, as the angel of Jehovah before them." (Cf. Isa. lv. 3, 4.)

The future Saviour of Israel was so entirely identified with the expected restoration of the Davidic dynasty, that all the unfulfilled hopes which had attached to the ancient monarchs, all the features which prophets and psalmists had ascribed to the perfect or ideal king, were transferred to the Messiah, and passages which expressed these hopes or ideals came to be recognised, as we gather from N. T. and elsewhere, as prophecies of the Messiah—*e.g.*, Psalms ii., xviii., xx., xlv., lxi., lxxii., cx.

The character and attributes of the Royal Saviour of Israel are set forth in such passages as those already referred to. He is the ideal King, perfectly endowed with all royal, physical, mental, moral, and spiritual qualities.

His government is absolutely righteous and beneficent at home; He is victorious abroad, and secures peace and dominion for Israel; in Dan. vii. 14, He attains to the universal empire as "a son of man," but He is also the symbol of the Divine Presence with Israel—Immanuel (Isa. vii. 14, viii. 8). While the O. T. does not expressly ascribe a superhuman or strictly divine character to Messiah—even the El Gibbor (E.V. "Mighty God") of Isa. ix. 6, can be paralleled from epithets applied to human kings: *e.g.*, 2 Sam. xiv. 17; Isa. x. 21 probably refers to ix. 6—the terms in which He is spoken of convey an almost irresistible suggestion of His superhuman nature. The hopes and aspirations of the Messianic prophecies could never be realised in a mere man; the two ideas, of Jehovah as the Divine King of Israel, and of the King who was to be his perfect representative upon earth might at first seem parallel, but they really converged, and coalesced at last; similarly in His functions as Saviour of Israel the Messiah is the representative of Jehovah, and Jehovah is often spoken of as delivering Israel Himself, personally and directly; He also is the Saviour of Israel (Isa. xl.-xlvi. *passim—e.g.*, xl. 9-11, xlix. 26), "I Jehovah am the Saviour." (Cf. Jer. xiv. 8; Zech. ix. 12-17; Zeph. iii. 15-17.) Thus the ideas of the Divine King and Saviour on the one hand, and of His representative on earth, the Messianic King Saviour, naturally met and merged at last in the doctrine of the Incarnation. Even in the O. T., in

Mal. iii. 1, the Lord (Adonai), the Messenger of the Covenant, is not clearly distinguished from Jehovah Himself.

The Messiah as the instrument of God's gracious purposes for Israel and His judgments on the Gentiles, is the counterpart of the Assyrian kings and of Nebuchadnezzar, whom God had commissioned to execute His judgments upon Israel and its neighbours. The close though antithetic relation between the office of these Gentile monarchs and that of the Davidic Messiah is illustrated by the fact that, when the deliverance of Israel is to be effected by the Gentile Cyrus, he also is called Jehovah's Messiah (Isa. xlv. 1).

At times, as we have partly shown above (Micah v. 2), the connection of the Messianic King with David is only implied, or even left doubtful (Isa. xxxii. 1, xxxiii. 17; Zech. ix. 9-11). In some passages the functions of the Messiah are transferred to a number of princes or rulers—*e.g.*, Micah v. 5, " seven shepherds and eight chiefs."

However, all these varying ideas concerning the Messiah agree in the essential point of ascribing the final salvation of Israel, and therefore of the world (cf. § 33), to a Monarch who shall be the divinely accredited representative of Jehovah, who is commissioned by Him to deliver His people from foreign enemies, and to rule them righteously in prosperity and peace. These aspects of the Messiah's person and work are almost always combined with his connection with the Davidic dynasty.

ii. MESSIAH AS PROPHET.—The suffering Servant of

Jehovah (Isa. lii. 13—liii. 12). Though the term Messiah strictly describes Him as King, yet it has been extended to include other aspects of His person and work. As in the last centuries of the monarchy of Judah the prophets eclipsed the kings, we naturally expect to find the expected Saviour is to be prophet as well as king. Indeed, the two functions of prophet and civil ruler were actually combined in Moses (Deut. xviii. 15), in Samuel (1 Sam. iii. 20) and, to some extent, even in Saul (1 Sam. x. 11, ff.). Acts ii. 30 is quite in harmony with the spirit of the O. T. in speaking of David as a prophet.

Moreover, the prophets attempted, by direct spiritual means or indirect influence, the same tasks that Gentile kings and the Israelite Messiah accomplished by the sword. Jeremiah's commission, for instance, is "to be set" over the nations and kingdoms, "to root out, pull down, destroy and throw down, to build, and to plant" (i. 10). On the other hand the Messianic King of Isa. xi. 1-10 has the prophetic gifts of Jehovah's "spirit of wisdom and understanding, of counsel and might, of knowledge and of the fear of Jehovah" (xi. 3).

Accordingly, in Isa. xl.-lxvi., the Messianic King recedes into the background, and the deliverer appears as the Servant of Jehovah entrusted with a prophetic mission first to Israel and then to mankind (xlix. 5, 6). Though this Servant sometimes stands for Israel or the believing Remnant (cf. § 10, iii.), he is throughout a prophet, and when in lii. 13—liii. 12 he is individualised we have to note that the Saviour of Israel and of the world now appears as a prophet.

But the Servant of Jehovah will not redeem Israel merely by teaching and preaching. In the last days of the Jewish monarchy God's faithful servants had been conspicuous for their sufferings; Josiah had been cut off in the prime of his manhood, Jeremiah had been, for the greater part of his life, "despised and rejected of men." Isa. liii. 5-10 sees in the sufferings of the Righteous One a vicarious atonement for the sin of Israel: and the Servant of Jehovah delivers Israel from sin by His death. In Daniel we find both aspects of the Messiah—the conquering King, in the universal and eternal King who is almost identified with the Most High (vii. 14, 17); and the Sufferer, in Messiah the Prince (ix. 26) who is cut off.* (Cf., however, § 10, i., note, and iv.)

As the conception of Messiah as the ideal king led to a Messianic application of the Psalms dealing with the king and kingdom: so the idea of the vicarious suffering of the Messiah seems to have led to a similar application of Psalms dealing with the sufferings of the righteous. Hence in N. T., Psalms xxii., xxxv., xli., lxix., are recognised as Messianic and applied to Christ.

iii. THE MESSIAH AS THE TRUE ISRAEL.—We have seen in § 7, vii. that Isa. xl.-lxvi., with an elasticity which it is difficult for the modern Western mind to follow, sees in the Servant of Jehovah at once Israel (xliv. 1, 2, xlv. 4, xlix. 3; etc.), and the individual Saviour of Israel (lii. 1—liii. 12; etc.). The

* The A.V. translation of the next clause "but not for himself" is corrected by R.V. to "and shall have nothing"; marg. "there shall be none belonging to him."

Israel here is, for the most part, the true Israel of believers, the Remnant of the elder prophets (so apparently, xlix. 5. Cf. xlvi. 3). Thus the idea is suggested that the true Israel, which is ultimately to be co-extensive with the actual Israel, becomes one with the Messiah or Saviour of Israel and the world. Similarly, in the N. T., Christ is not only the Personal Saviour, but one with the Church as a vine with its branches (John xvi. 8), and a body with its limbs (1 Cor. xii. 27).

iv. THE MESSIAH AS PRIEST.—The royal and priestly functions were closely allied in the ancient world, and so in Israel we find David and subsequent kings sacrificing and exercising other priestly functions. Hence the kingly status of the Messiah almost implies His priesthood. But in the post-exilic period the title Messiah was extended to the High Priest (Lev. iv. 3, 5, 16; Dan. ix. 25, 26), as the highest authority in the Jewish state, as well as in the Jewish Church. Thus in Zechariah, even when Zerubbabel, the prince of the House of David, was governor for the Persians, and still therefore the civil head of the community, the high priest Joshua is placed on a level with him, and the two together are spoken of as the "two sons of oil"— *i.e.*, "anointed ones," or Messiahs (iv. 14)—and in the present Hebrew text of vi. 9-13 Jeremiah's prophecy of the branch is applied to the high priest Joshua. In the original text it is true, Zerubbabel is the branch, and Joshua sits at his right hand; but the alteration shows that at some period of post-exilic Judaism special stress was laid on the priestly character of the Messiah. So Psalm cx. depicts the Saviour of Israel as both civil ruler and priest.

11. New Heavens and New Earth.—At times the prophetic vision widens to a far horizon, where earth and heaven meet and blend so that the one can scarcely be distinguished from the other. Jehovah the Heavenly Saviour and the Messiah upon earth appear one and the same, § 10, i. : the vindication of Israel by its victory over the nations is combined with the resurrection of the dead and the final judgment, § 32 : the Day of Jehovah upon earth is ushered in by celestial portents (Hag. ii. 6), and Jehovah not only renews the face of Palestine (§ 9, v.), but creates a new heaven and a new earth (Isa. lxvi. 17, 22).

CHAPTER IV
JEHOVAH AS THE GOD OF ISRAEL

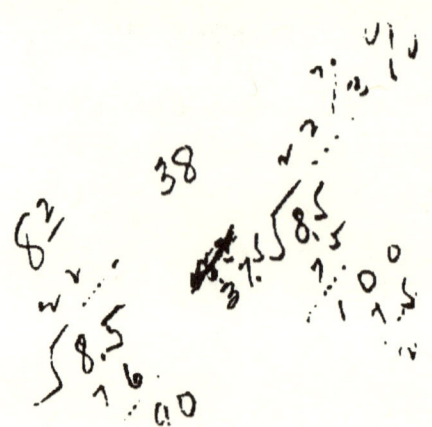

CHAPTER IV

JEHOVAH AS THE GOD OF ISRAEL

12. Names.—The relation of Jehovah to Israel is expressed by various names and titles. Both in ancient proper names and various passages we find Baal = Lord, (Ish-baal, cf. Hosea iii. 6), Melek = King, (Malchi-ram, cf. Isa. xliv. 6), Zur = Rock (Pedah-zur, cf. 2 Sam. xxii. 32), Ab = Father (Abi-ram, cf. Jer. xxxi. 9), used as names or titles of the God of Israel.

But the personal name of God, as the God of Israel, is now represented in the Hebrew Text of O. T. by the four consonants, YHWH. When the English Version attempts to reproduce this name they represent it by Jehovah, following an ancient misunderstanding (cf. below). The original pronunciation of this name is not certainly known, though it is generally supposed to have been Yahweh.* Its primitive etymology and significance are still more uncertain, (for the interpretation given in Ex. iii. 14, see § 37), and there is no reason to suppose that they were known in Israel during the historical period: consequently they are no more a

* Yahwe, Yahveh, Yahve, etc., are merely equivalent spellings of Yahweh. The use of J is a Germanism for Y. Cf. Preface.

part of O. T. Revelation, than the etymology of the word God is a part of English theology. YHWH (E. V. "Jehovah") was to the ordinary Israelite simply a proper name for the God he worshipped, as "God" now is to the Christian.

The loss of the pronunciation of YHWH was due to a peculiar use of another divine name, ADONAI (Lord). Under later Judaism an exaggerated reverence for the Most Sacred Name made the Jews to refrain from using YHWH, and substitute for it either ADONAI or ELOHIM. They were followed by the LXX. and Vulgate, and from the Vulgate the English versions adopted the habit of writing LORD or GOD for YHWH.

To secure the substitution of Adonai for YHWH in the public reading of O. T., the vowels of Adonai were attached to the four consonants YHWH as a *q'ri perpetuum*, or standing direction that Adonai should be read for YHWH.* When the Jewish tradition was unknown amongst Christians the consonants were mistakenly combined with the attached vowels; and, being slightly modified, the linguistically impossible form Jehovah was produced.

This Name is used to form the names of persons, either as prefix *JEHO* or affix *IAH*; and of places, especially altars—*e.g.*, Jehovah-jireh, -nissi, -shalom. But its most significant and frequent combination is YHWH Ç'BAOTH, E.V. "LORD of Hosts," N.T. "Lord of Sabaoth" (Rom. ix. 29; James v. 4). This title is specially common in Amos, Isaiah (both parts),

* If Adonai immediately precedes YHWH, the latter takes the vowels of ELOHIM, hence E.V. "GOD."

Jeremiah, Haggai, Zechariah (both parts) and Malachi; in 1 Sam. iv. 4; 2 Sam. vi. 2, it seems specially connected with the ark. The title is altogether wanting in Judges, in Ezekiel, the Pentateuch and Joshua, in Joel, Obadiah, and Jonah; and with the exception of a few Psalms, and some passages which Chronicles borrows from Samuel, "the Lord of Hosts" does not occur at all in the Hagiographa.

The term "hosts" has been variously explained—of the actual Israelite armies, the stars, the angelic hosts, the elemental powers. Probably at different periods each of these interpretations was current among the Jews themselves. Each interpretation would signify the champion of Israel against its enemies, whether by means of the arms of Israel itself, or by divine forces which dispensed with human co-operation. This sense would harmonise with the apparent connection with the ark, which in early times was carried into battle as the symbol of Jehovah's presence with the armies of His people (2 Sam. xi. 11).

13. Anthropomorphism and Anthropopathism.—According to the necessities of human thought and language, there is much anthropomorphism and anthropopathism in O. T. We read of Jehovah's eyes, nostrils, ears, mouth, arms, feet, fingers, etc. He sees, smells, hears, laughs, strikes, stands, sits, walks, etc. Sometimes Jehovah is even spoken of in terms borrowed from animal life; He has wings; He flies and roars. His moral and mental attributes are also expressed in the same terms as those of man.

O. T. does not, however, intend to transfer to God the limitations and defects of human life and character; such language merely serves to make the divine nature, attributes, and operations approximately intelligible to men.

14. The Bond between Jehovah and Israel.
i. ELECTION AND DIVINE SOVEREIGNTY.—The history of Israel is initiated by God's choice of the nation; is controlled throughout by His purpose; and leads up at last, in spite of sin, and failure, and suffering, to the realisation of that abiding purpose. Jehovah is the King of Israel, and the Lord and owner of Palestine (cf. § 18, i.). This election created a relation which is set forth, not only as that between king and subjects, but also as that between Providence and the objects of its care, between father and son, husband and wife, patron and client, and between the two parties to a covenant.

ii. PROVIDENCE.—O. T. recognises the living presence and immediate working of God in all operations and processes of nature, and all events of national and individual history.

iii. FATHERHOOD.—From the time of Hosea xi. 1 onwards the prophets often use the term "Father" to describe the relation of Jehovah to Israel. In using this figure O. T. is not concerned with the way in which the relation of father and son originates; it does not suggest any essential, almost physical, bond, which might seem to exist independently of any divine choice (cf. 1). The term sets forth the actual existing relation between Jehovah and Israel; His authority over and affection for His people.

iv. MARRIAGE.—In Hosea ii., iii.; Jer. ii. 2; Isa. liv. 5, 6; Ezek. xvi., Jehovah is spoken of as the husband of Israel; and the same figure is implied in the constant description of idolatry as adultery, or going a-whoring after other gods. This figure must be understood in the light of woman's dependent position in the East. So in Ezek. xvi., Jerusalem was helpless and forlorn when Jehovah espoused her out of pure compassion. This figure chiefly emphasises the free choice of Jehovah, the unswerving fidelity owed to Him by His people, and the entire dependence of Israel. It may also imply, to a very limited extent, Israel's free acceptance of Jehovah, "the love of her espousals" (Jer. ii. 2).

v. ISRAEL THE "GER" OR "CLIENT" OF JEHOVAH.— In a few passages (Psalms xv. 1, xxxix. 12) Israel is spoken of as Jehovah's *Ger*—*i.e.*, a resident alien under the protection of the chief of a tribe. This figure again emphasises the free grace of Jehovah and the helpless dependence of Israel.

vi. THE COVENANT.—A covenant was the mutual agreement of two or more contracting parties upon conditions profitable to both; it did not necessarily imply equality between the contracting parties, for it is even applied to the terms imposed by a conqueror upon his defeated enemy, or by a suzerain upon his vassal (Ezek. xvii. 13). In making a covenant with Israel, Jehovah declared His gracious purposes towards His people, and the conditions upon which they might enjoy His promised blessings; they, on their part, undertook to faithfully observe all His commands. As far as Jehovah was concerned a covenant did not greatly differ from a solemn promise made by Him to His chosen.

In Gen.—2 Kings, the earliest history of Israel has for its epochs a series of covenants; with Noah after the Flood (Gen. ix.); with Abraham, when Canaan was promised to his descendants (Gen. xv. xvii.); at Sinai, in connection with the giving of the Law, (Exod. xxxiv. 10; Deut. v. 2); under Joshua, after the Conquest of Canaan (Josh. xxiv. 25); under Josiah, in recognition of the authority of Deuteronomy (2 Kings xxiii. 3). Judges and Samuel record no covenants between Jehovah and Israel; but the promise of permanence to the Davidic dynasty is spoken of as an everlasting covenant in 2 Sam. xxiii. 5. One of the oldest sections of the Pentateuch (Exod. xx. 20—xxiii. 33) is called the "Book of the Covenant" (xxiv. 7); Hosea ii. 18, vi. 7, viii. 1; Jer. xi. 10, etc., xxxi. 31, ff.; Ezek. xx. 37, etc.; Isa. xlii. 6, etc., emphasise this aspect of Jehovah's relation to Israel. At the close of the O. T. history, Ezra and Nehemiah established the Levitical Law as the code and canon of Judaism (Neh. x. 29, ff.) by a covenant.* These covenants have many differences of detail and circumstance; but they agree in substance. Jehovah promises prosperity to Israel or its representatives on condition of obedience to His revealed will; Israel promises to observe this condition, though the promise is sometimes taken for granted and not stated. In such cases the covenant is concluded simply by a declaratory act on the part of Jehovah; it is offered to Israel or the Patriarchs, and its accept-

* The word "covenant," however, is not used here.

ance is assumed. In other cases the conclusion of a covenant is virtually the acceptance by Israel of the terms offered in the law and the prophets.

15. The Moral Attributes of Jehovah.—As moral attributes can only be manifested in connection with an object, these attributes are revealed in the dealings of Jehovah with Israel. Accordingly O. T. is not so much interested in what Jehovah is in Himself, as in what He is in His relations to Israel. His righteousness, truth, etc., are not so much abstract attributes of His essential nature, as modes of His action with regard to His people. And, again, while ultimately as a matter of abstract theology, there is no standard for God but Himself, in the practical understanding and application of these truths it is always assumed that the divine standard of righteousness answers to the highest human ideals. It transcends and corrects them, but does not essentially contradict or reverse them.

i. TRUSTWORTHINESS AND SELF-CONSISTENCY.—He shows righteousness (*çedeq, çdaqa*), as acting in conformity with the true standard of conduct—*i.e.*, His Revelation of Himself and His Will. This standard is reflected, though partially and imperfectly, in the human standards, based on men's moral instincts. He shows faithfulness (*emuna*) by persisting in His purposes and fulfilling His promises, and truth (*emeth*) by the fact that His utterances express His thought, feeling, and intention. These divine qualities are specially manifested in the persistency of Jehovah's choice of Israel (Isa. xli. 8-10), and by His faithfulness to His covenant (Ezek. xxxvii. 26 ; cf. xxxvi. 21).

ii. BENEVOLENCE. — He loves Israel, and shows "mercy" (E.V. for *ḥesed*), a disposition to be bountiful and gracious beyond anything that can be claimed from Him; He shows tender compassion and pitifulness (*raḥam raḥamim raḥum*, E.V. "tender love," "compassion," "pity," "full of compassion"), He pities and spares (*raḥam, ḥus ḥamal*), is long-suffering (*erek appayim*). He not only forgives (*salaḥ, nasa l'*), but is eager that His people should repent and be forgiven (Hosea xi. 8, 9; Ezek. xviii. 32, xxxiii. 11).

iii. JUSTICE.—His justice is part of His righteousness (*çedeq*); He judges (*din, shaphat*) righteously between man and man, assigning to each his due, his "judgment" (*mishpat*). What is thus due is determined by the fact that Jehovah is not only righteous Himself, but requires righteousness in Israel. Hence He rewards right doing, and punishes sin; He is angry with the sinner. Moreover, He is jealous of His rights, and counts it sin that Israel confounds Him with other gods, and worships other gods in addition to or instead of Himself.

iv. GLORY (KABOD); MAJESTY (GAON); SANCTITY (QODESH); cf. § 17.—These attributes serve to express His supernatural power, splendour, and exaltation, which are, on the one hand, part of the manifestation of Jehovah to Israel; and yet, on the other hand, tend to forbid any close or constant fellowship of Israel with Jehovah.

v. THE NAME.—The sum of the divine attributes of Jehovah and of what is known of His will and working make up the divine name, or revealed character and purpose of God.

16. Jehovah's Revelation of Himself. i. THEO-
PHANIES.—Jehovah Himself is not immediately *seen*
by men, though, like Isaiah (vi.) and Ezekiel (i.), they
may have visions of Him; or, like Moses (Exod.
xxiv.), may behold some manifestation of His presence. The statement that Moses and the elders " saw
the God of Israel " is apparently qualified by the fact
that no further account is given of what they saw
than that they saw the pavement under His feet.
Jehovah, however, constantly speaks directly to men.
As a rule, He is seen and heard by representatives of
Israel.

ii. THE SUPERNATURAL ORGANS OF REVELATION.—
(*a*) *The Spirit* (*ruah*). Jehovah makes known His
will to men by His Spirit, and by His Spirit they are
impelled to fulfil His purposes, and are endowed with
necessary strength and wisdom. The warrior is inspired to fight (Judg. vi. 34); the husbandman to
cultivate the soil (Isa. xxviii. 23-29); the artisan
to exercise his handicraft (Exod. xxxi. 3); the priest
and prophet to announce the divine will (2 Chron.
xv. 1), and the king to govern (1 Sam. xvi. 13).

(*b*) *The Word.*—The instrument of the divine
working in Creation and Providence is also spoken of
as "the Word," and the same idea is implied when
God *speaks* or *commands*, and His purposes are
forthwith accomplished (Gen. i.; Isa. xlviii. 13;
Psalm xxxiii. 6, 9, cxlvii. 18, 19, cxlviii. 5). The
" Word of Jehovah " is constantly said to come to the
prophets (Jer. i. 2, etc. Cf. the references to God's
voice in Deut. iv. 12; 1 Sam. iii. 4; 1 Kings
xix. 11, ff.). The later developments of the usage

of the term "Word" in the Apocrypha, Philo, etc., connect it with the Logos doctrine of St. John. Another line of connection is indicated by the later Jewish doctrine of the "Word" in the Targums, Talmud, etc.

(c) *Wisdom* (*ḥokma*).—The wisdom of God would naturally be thought of as primarily an attribute of the divine nature, guiding His Spirit and shaping His Word. From being a divine attribute, it becomes a gift from God to man—*e.g.*, Solomon, 1 Kings iii. 28. But in Proverbs and Job the doctrine of wisdom takes special forms. As against the conception of Jehovah consulting with the angels—the host of heaven (1 Kings xxii. 19, 20), the seraphim (Isa. vi.), the sons of God (Job i. 6, ii. 1); Prov. viii. 22-31 depicts wisdom as the eldest son and most ancient possession of Jehovah, His associate and master-workman (30 R. V.) in creation. Moreover, wisdom is the source of all honourable human activity and true prosperity (Prov. viii. 14-18). In Job xxviii. wisdom is a mystery, unfathomable by man, and is even depicted as a matter which God investigates, discovers, and then reveals :

Whence then cometh wisdom? . . .
It is hid from the eyes of all living, . . .
Destruction and death say
We have heard a rumour thereof with our ears,
God understandeth the way thereof,
He knoweth the place thereof,
He looketh to the ends of the earth,
He seeth under the whole heaven, . . .
Then did He see and declare it,

He established it, yea, and searched it out,
And unto man He said:
Behold the fear of the Lord, that is wisdom,
And to depart from evil is understanding.
                                            (20-28).
Here and elsewhere wisdom is parallel to, and partly synonymous with, understanding (*bina*).

There is an obvious connection between the passages in Job and Proverbs. And this connection emphasises the contrast between the abstract quality or force in Job—which is depicted almost as independent of God and needing to be sought and found by Him—and the free personification of Proverbs. The later development of the doctrine of wisdom in Ecclesiasticus and the Wisdom of Solomon is rather on the lines of Proverbs. (Cf., in N. T., Matt. xi. 19; Luke vii. 35, xi. 49.)

(*d*) *The Angels.*—The divine activity is not only spoken of as exercised directly and through the Spirit, Word, and Wisdom, but also through subordinate supernatural beings, by whom He is surrounded, as by a heavenly court, variously described as the host of Heaven, the sons of God, the cherubim, the seraphim, and more generally as angels (*Malakhim*—messengers). Nothing is said as to the origin of these beings, and attention is directed to their functions rather than to their nature.

The *Host of Heaven* form the council of Jehovah in 1 Kings xxii. 19, and his Hosts are spoken of in Psalm ciii. 21. (Cf. Dan. vii. 10.)

Sons of God.—A similar position is occupied in Job i. 6, ii. 1 by the sons of God (Bnê Elohim), cf. xxxviii. 7. The term is parallel to "sons of the Prophets," and denotes subordinates owning some community or similarity of nature and function to their superior (cf. Elohim, Psalm viii. 5).

The Angel of Jehovah, The Angel of Elohim.—In the older documents attention is concentrated upon one special, pre-eminent angel, called the angel of Jehovah, or of Elohim. In the same passages He is at one time identified with Jehovah, and at another distinguished from Him—*e.g.*, cf. Judg. vi. 11, 12, 20, 21 with 14, 16, 23; and xiii. 15-21, with 22, 23. The angel of Jehovah is, therefore, almost rather a theophany or divine manifestation, than a messenger. He seems to be represented as the manifestation of that special presence of Jehovah with Israel, which was symbolised by the ark.*

Cherubim.—These appear as guarding Eden with fiery swords (Gen. iii. 24). Figures representing cherubim were used to ornament the curtains of the Tabernacle (Ex. xxxvi. 8) and the walls of the Temple (1 Kings vi. 28, 29), and to cover the Mercy Seat (Exod. xxx., xxxvii.). Such figures symbolise the attendance of the cherubim on Jehovah in His heavenly Temple. In Ezek. ix., x.; Psalms xviii. 10, lxxx. 1, xcix. 1, the cherubim are spoken of as supporting and carrying the throne of Jehovah. They are generally represented as winged or flying; Ezekiel's description is exceedingly elaborate and complicated, but it was probably not intended to apply to the cherubim generally. The etymology and history of the word are uncertain.

* Smend, 42.

JEHOVAH AS THE GOD OF ISRAEL 109

Seraphim.—These are only mentioned in Isa. vi. 1, where they appear in attendance on Jehovah. The word elsewhere (Num. xxi. 8; Isa. xiv. 29, xxx. 6) means a fiery serpent.

Angels generally, and individual Angels.—With slight exceptions (Gen. xix. 1, xxxii. 1; 1 Kings xiii. 18) the references to angels in the earlier literature are confined to the angel of Jehovah, or of Elohim. The "an angel of Jehovah" in A.V. of various passages should be corrected to "the angel," as R. V. Marg. Angels generally are mentioned in Job iv. 18; Psalm xci. 11, etc. In Zech. two or three angels, including the angel of Jehovah, communicate and interpret the divine message to the prophet. But in Daniel, angels — other than the angel of Jehovah — are mentioned by name, Gabriel (viii. 16, ix. 21), Michael (x. 13, etc.). Michael is "the prince" or guardian angel of Israel, and fights with angelic allies against the "princes" or guardian angels of the nations hostile to Israel (x. 20, 21, xii. 1). The doctrine of the angels was greatly elaborated by later Judaism, from which we learn the names of numerous members of the angelic hierarchy.

Satan, Adversary, first appears as one of the Bnê Elohim in Job, and may be compared with the lying spirit in 1 Kings xxii. 22. He is thus subordinate to Jehovah, and even in a sense one of His ministering angels, working with His permission, and even as His agent. In Zech. iii. 1, 2 (cf. Psalm cix. 6) he appears as the accuser of Joshua the High Priest; his accusations are not refuted, but he is rebuked for wishing to hinder the free operation of divine grace and mercy. 1 Chron. xxi. 1 substitutes Satan for Jehovah (2 Sam. xxiv. 1) as the author of the temptation to David to number Israel. O. T. does not identify Satan with the serpent who tempted Eve.

Devils.—O. T. has hardly any references to evil angels other than Satan. Various objects of popular superstition are mentioned; he-goats, R.V., or satyrs R.V. Marg. (Lev. xvii. 7; 2 Chron. xi. 15), *se'irim*, demons—false gods (Deut. xxxii. 17; Psalm cvi. 37), *shedim*. But these passages do not seem to sanction any belief in the real existence of such beings. The "evil angels," *malakhe ra'im* (cf. Psalm lxxviii. 49) are not to be distinguished from the ordinary angels; they are not evil in nature, but inflict evil—*i.e.*, punishment upon man.

iii. TRANSCENDENTALISM.—To thus refer the divine utterance and activity to intermediate beings and qualities, instead of immediately to God Himself, serves to emphasise the solitary and ineffable majesty of the Most High. It also tended, however, to obscure the divine immanence and the possibility of direct fellowship between God and man. It belongs chiefly to the last period of O.T. Revelation, when the Jews had become fully conscious that Jehovah ruled, not only Israel, but all nations and the whole universe, so that the growing sense of the power and majesty of Jehovah seemed to set Him alone, aloof, and apart from man.

iv. FORESHADOWINGS OF THE DOCTRINE OF THE TRINITY. — O. T. use of the terms word, spirit, wisdom, etc., is originally anthropomorphic; the action and life of God are described and illustrated in terms of the faculties and actions of men. Even when the Word, etc., are spoken of as if they possessed a certain independence, and could stand in a kind of personal relation to God, such language still follows the analogy of phrases in which a man is said "to commune with his own heart." O. T., however, shows a predilection for such language, and develops the usage to an extent which indicates that to define the Godhead as a single personality does not satisfy the data of revelation. This O. T. usage found its natural issue in the Christian doctrine of the Trinity. But that doctrine is still more clearly foreshadowed in the peculiar position assigned by O. T. to the angel of Jehovah, as a supernatural being who is at one and the same time virtually identical with Jehovah, and yet capable of personal relations with Him.

v. REVELATION IN NATURE AND HISTORY.—As Jehovah is Creator and Ruler of the Universe, all nature is a revelation. This is recognised in such passages as Psalm xix. 1-6 :

"The heavens declare the glory of God,
The firmament showeth his handywork."

Cf. Psalm. viii. 3. The same idea underlies God's answer to Job in Job xxxviii.-xli.

Similarly, God's moral government of the world by His Providence implies that the courses and events of history are a further revelation. This is recognised by the presence of the historical books in O. T., and by the constant appeal of the other books to Jehovah's manifestation of Himself in history. Note especially Psalms lxxviii., cv.-cvii., which celebrate

God's dealings with Israel. While O. T. chiefly dwells on the revelation given in the history of Israel, yet it also recognises that such a revelation is to be found in all history. This would necessarily be the case with all nations in any way connected with Israel, but it is also implied that God's hand may be traced in the history of Gentile nations considered in themselves. For instance, Amos ix. 7 expressly places the emigration of the Philistines from Caphtor and the Syrians from Kir on a level with the Exodus from Egypt.

Moreover man, the meeting point of nature and history, is made in the image and likeness of God (Gen. i. 26), and is given dominion over all beneath him. Hence human life, both in its relation to nature, and in individuals, and societies, and their mutual dealings, must constitute in some way a revelation.

vi. HUMAN AGENTS OF REVELATION, INSPIRATION; cf. § 4, i.—We have already seen that the direct and immediate revelation of Jehovah to Israel is almost always through the representatives of the nation; this principle also holds good of the revelation made through supernatural agents, and through nature and history.

(a) *The Nation.* — When Israel is faithful, its national life is a revelation of God's will and character; so also is the punishment of Israel's disobedience. Similarly the individual Israelite of every class—king, prophet, priest, farmer, artisan—in some measure reveals Jehovah if he yields to the divine inspiration.

(b) *The King.*—More especially the king or judge,

as the agent through whom Jehovah bestows the blessings of social order and victory over enemies, represents Jehovah to Israel.

(c) *The Prophet.*—The Prophetic order, however, was pre-eminently the channel of divine revelation. The special function of the prophet was to represent Jehovah—to be His messenger to Israel. The regular ritual was fixed and might be learned from the priests; but Jehovah had commands and counsel for all the unforeseen contingencies of national and individual life. Jehovah's organ for such commands and counsel was the prophet. Accordingly all the new departures of national life are authorised by prophets; therefore Abraham (Gen. xx. 7), Moses (Deut. xviii. 18), Samuel, David (Acts ii. 30), are all recognised as prophets. Ahijah announces the division of Israel into two kingdoms (1 Kings xi. 29), and the fall of Jeroboam's dynasty (xiv. 7, ff.), and Elijah, the overthrow of the house of Omri (xxi. 22). The captivity and return are announced by the later prophets. Similarly the great spiritual revelations are contained in the prophetical books; a recognition of this prophetic office led to the ascription of the Pentateuch to Moses, and of the historical books, Joshua—Kings, to the prophets.

(d) *The Priest.*—In the case of the Priests the representation of Jehovah to Israel was not their most characteristic function; nevertheless, they were His representatives, as conveying to the people, in their blessing, the assurance of the divine favour and acceptance (Num. vi. 22-27), and as teaching Jehovah's will by communicating and interpreting the Torah (Deut. xxxiii. 10). In earlier times priestly functions seem to have been wider and to have virtually included those of the later prophets; priests not only laid down the law as to conduct and worship, but also gave counsel in emergencies, by Urim and Thummim, and otherwise (1 Sam. xxviii. 6, xxx. 8). But the priest, as priest, never conveys Jehovah's commands for any great new departure, nor does he communicate any important new revelation.

vii. METHODS OF REVELATION.— Perhaps the best Hebrew equivalent, in the older literature, for our term "revelation," would be Torah (E.V., "Law," R.V. Mg., "instruction"). Torah is in the first instance a revelation of the divine will, on some special point made through a priest or prophet. This communication of the divine will is made in ancient times by lot (Urim and Thummim, and Ephod were probably forms of lot)—*e.g.*, in the cases of Achan (Josh. vii. 14), Saul (1 Sam. x. 21), Saul and Jonathan (xiv. 41). The recourse to lots is not sanctioned by the prophets or the later legislation. Revelations were also made by *dreams* in the night; by *visions—i.e.*, impressions made upon the mind during an abnormal mental condition of trance or ecstasy; by *types—i.e.*, a divine use of a natural object as an image or parable of the divine message. At times it is said that a *voice* came to the prophet (1 Kings xix.). Sometimes the revelation is received through an *angel*, especially in the books of Zechariah and Daniel, where, however, the chief function of the angels is to interpret visions seen by the prophets. For the most part, however, it is simply said that Jehovah spoke to the

JEHOVAH AS THE GOD OF ISRAEL 115

prophet, or that the word of Jehovah came to the prophet.

O. T. does not tell us how the prophets were assured of the divine origin of the dreams, visions, voices, or word of Jehovah. Probably the trance or ecstasy was regarded as a token of inspiration; but the almost entire absence of any appeal to external marks of inspiration indicates that the prophetic assurance rested chiefly upon an inner spiritual sense of fellowship with Jehovah.

Similarly the O. T. lays down no clear rules by which the people might be assured of a prophet's inspiration, though numerous cases occur in which the true prophets were contradicted by others who also claimed to speak in the name of Jehovah—*e.g.*, Micaiah ben-Imlah by Ahab's prophets (1 Kings xxii.), Jeremiah by Hananiah (Jer. xxviii.). Jeremiah xxviii. (8, 9) indeed suggests that a prophecy of evil is more likely to be true than prophecy of good; but this canon is obviously of special and limited application. Again Deut. xviii. 21, 22, makes fulfilled prediction the credentials of a true prophet; but this test might often be valid, and yet, unless used with much discrimination, prove altogether misleading. Moreover Elijah on Carmel (1 Kings xviii.), and Isaiah, with Ahaz (vii. 11) and Hezekiah (xxxviii. 7), offer signs as proofs of their divine mission. But for the most part, the impression given by the O. T. is that a prophet's most convincing credentials were the self-verifying effects his words produced on the hearts and consciences of his hearers.

vii. RECORD OF REVELATION. *Canon. Cf.* § 5, xi.

—The divine acts and utterances which constitute O. T. revelation were, in the first instance, given to individuals, or to the nation through individuals, in reference to the special circumstances of various periods and crises. Sometimes a prophet, as in Jer. xxxvi., might communicate his message in writing; but the writing was rather a letter or written address, than an attempt after literary permanence—the revelation was so far complete when the message had reached the ears or eyes for which it was first intended.

But these messages were soon felt to embody permanent truth; and God's dealings with Israel were seen to have a permanent significance. Hence, the prophets or their disciples committed the inspired words to writing, and histories of Israel began. The preservation of these records shows that they were naturally cherished with affection and reverence; otherwise O. T. lays down no doctrine of prophetic and historic Scripture.

The legislation stands on a different footing. Each ordinance was originally a divine torah addressed to some special need. Then as each prophecy embodied a permanent principle, so each legal decision furnished a precedent. Customary law might long remain oral, but convenience ultimately caused its reduction to writing. Moreover, the authority of a legal code needed to be definitely accepted and established. Thus the successive editions of the Mosaic torah obtained canonical authority by means of solemn covenants; Deuteronomy under Josiah (2 Kings xxiii.), the Levitical law under Nehemiah (x.).

The doctrine of our present O. T. canon is necessarily not a part of O. T. theology, for the formation of a canon implies that the revelation is closed and complete. Moreover, the limits of the O. T. canon amongst the Jews were still under discussion at the beginning of the Christian era; and the Christian Church is still hopelessly divided as to the O. T. canon, the Protestant Churches rejecting a number of books received by the remainder of Western Christendom. Thus the attempts to fix this canon are far too late to be received as part of the revelation given by God in O. T.

ix. THE SCOPE OF REVELATION. —Nevertheless, in the present work, we assume the canon of the Protestant Churches, which, at any rate, has the advantage of only including those books which are universally accepted. Even within these limits God's revelation to Israel is seen to be of immense variety and comprehensiveness. God reveals, through a long series of centuries, His will and purpose for the past, present, and future, and also for all classes of Israelites and all circumstances and occasions of life.

While N. T. is the literature of a single unique period, O. T. belongs to a long succession of critical epochs; N. T. is the account of a new faith in its first stages; O. T. enables us to trace religious ideas through centuries of growth. N. T. concentrates attention on the personal religious life, and all its heroes are religious teachers. O. T. sets forth the will and purpose of God as regards the nation; its heroes are not merely prophets and priests: they are patriarchs, shepherds, kings, like Abraham, Job,

David, and Saul; queens like Esther; slaves and statesmen, like Joseph and Nehemiah; simple women, like Ruth and Naomi. Divine guidance and grace are sought and given as to the choice of a home or a wife, the birth of children, the gathering and spending of worldly gear, the organisation and government of the state in its home and foreign politics; in short, all the varied interests of life are depicted as consecrated and inspired.

The contents of the canon further illustrate this comprehensiveness. O. T. is not the text-book of a church, but the literature of a nation, its legal codes, its maxims of worldly wisdom, its poems and romances, its histories, its prayers and hymns and sermons, even its scepticism. Indeed, as we have seen, even the polemics of opposing theological schools lie side by side in O. T. When the Holy Spirit constrained a half unconscious Church to group all these into one sacred volume, He proclaimed emphatically that no earnest and honest movement of human thought or life was common or unclean.

This variety of Jehovah's manifestation of Himself to Israel suggests the exact adaptation of the divine messages to various needs and changing circumstances. Threats and promises are never arbitrary; the execution of a threat may be averted by penitence (cf. also the apparently unconditional prediction of the ruin of Nineveh in Jonah iii. 4, and God's repentance in iii. 10), and the fulfilment of a promise may be forfeited by sin. Every advance in human conduct and condition involved a fuller and more blessed revelation of God. Thus in attempting to appreciate

O. T. teaching as to the divine nature, we cannot afford to lay undue stress even on its most important formulæ and most sublime passages; only when we try to grasp something of the marvellous variety and comprehensiveness of O. T. do we begin to understand what is meant by " Jehovah, the God of Israel."

CHAPTER V

ISRAEL AS THE PEOPLE OF JEHOVAH

CHAPTER V

ISRAEL AS THE PEOPLE OF JEHOVAH

17. Sanctity.—The term used to denote acts, persons, places, times, specially devoted to Jehovah and His worship, is QADOSH (E.V., "holy"). So *qodesh* (E.V., "holiness") is used of the quality of being thus devoted, and various verbal forms of *qdsh* are used in a corresponding sense. The connotation of the modern word "holy" is, as a rule, so different from that of *qadosh*, that it is misleading to use "holy" as its regular equivalent. Acts, etc., specially connected with worship or with man's relation to God are often called "religious" in modern English, and this would often be a fair equivalent of *qadosh*; but perhaps the word whose usage most closely corresponds to *qadosh* is "sacred." Hence, wherever possible, we shall represent *qadosh*, by "sacred."

But *qadosh* is also applied to Jehovah as the object of religious worship (Isa. vi. 3); He is Himself styled *qadosh*; in this connection the term may be rendered "divine"* as in our "divine being," "divine service."

Note.—As, however, the root *qdsh* is not peculiar to Hebrew, but is used in the sense of "religious," "sacred," by the Semitic peoples generally, certain

* Skinner's *Ezekiel*, 114.

Hebrew usages of the root are survivals of ancient Semitic heathenism, and have no connection with revealed religion. For instance *qedesha* is used for prostitute, because such persons were sacred in heathen religion.

18. Sacred Places. i. THE LAND OF ISRAEL.—Though in the earlier history Jehovah is specially connected with Horeb (Exod. iii. 1; Deut. i. 6) and Sinai (Exod. xix; Deut. xxxiii. 2; Judg. v. 5; Psalm lxviii. 8, 17); yet for the most part Palestine was specially the possession of Jehovah, the place where He dwelt and manifested Himself to His worshippers. Palestine is His inheritance (1 Sam. xxvi. 19), His house (Hosea viii. 1, ix. 15), His vineyard (Isa. i.-v.). Possibly on account of the early loss of the territory east of the Jordan, the sacred land is limited in Ezek. xlvii. 18; Josh. xxii. 19, to the western territory. Similarly, in later times, a special sanctity attached to Judæa in comparison with Galilee and, *a fortiori*, Samaria.

Jehovah's possession of Palestine does not, of course, originate with its occupation by Israel. Israel did not conquer Canaan for Jehovah; but Canaan was His possession, which He gave to His people.

ii. SACRED CHARACTER OF OWNERSHIP OF LAND. (*Doctrine of Property*).—Not only was the whole land Jehovah's gift to the nation, but also the inheritance of each tribe, clan, and family was a direct gift from Jehovah; hence the division by lot in Joshua. These inheritances were therefore inalienable. Hence the law of Jubilee (Lev. xxv., xxvi.) deprives the owner of land of the right of free sale. He can only dispose of a temporary usufruct, and the reversion is secured to the family. Similarly it is provided that land shall not pass from one tribe to another by a mixed marriage (Num. xxvi., xxvii., xxxvi.; Josh. xvii. 3). The collective rights of the clan in the land are further asserted by charging it with certain dues for the benefit of the poor (Lev. xix. 9, 10); and the rights of Jehovah are recognised in the provision made for the priesthood. The proper treatment of the soil, by leaving it fallow in the sabbatical year, and the year of Jubilee, is also constituted a religious duty.

As, after the conquest, land was the most important and permanent species of property, the land laws constitute a doctrine of property, as the gift of Jehovah, charged with the relief of the needy and the maintenance of all good works. Moreover, the principle is implied that the holder of property is to be careful of the rights and needs of succeeding generations. Both the prophets and the legislative codes try to secure that every free Israelite family, as a unit of the sacred nation, shall have its share in the sacred land.

iii. THE ANCIENT SANCTUARIES OR HIGH PLACES.— The sanctity of Palestine, as the place where Jehovah specially manifested Himself to Israel, is shown in the Pentateuch and Joshua by the theophanies at Beersheba (Gen. xlvi. 1), Bethel (Gen. xxviii. 19, xxxv. 14, 15); Gerar (xx. 2, xxvi. 2); Gilgal (Josh. v. 13); Mamre (Gen. xviii. 1); Moriah (xxii. 2, etc.), within the limits of Palestine. Although the patriarchal history narrates theophanies outside

Palestine, it does not specially connect them with any definite locality; when God appears to Jacob in Padan-Aram He styles Himself the God of Bethel (Gen. xxxi. 13).

The Palestinian scenes of these theophanies are found, for the most part, amongst the "high places," which are referred to in Samuel, Kings, and the Prophets as the seats of popular worship. As their connection, in many cases, with the patriarchal history implies, they were sanctuaries of Jehovah, so that Solomon sacrificed at Gibeon, because it was "the great high place" (1 Kings iii. 4). The worship, however, at these sanctuaries became corrupt; Jehovah was worshipped under the form of idols— *e.g.*, the calves at Bethel and Dan—and in combination with other deities. Hence, the prophets of the eighth century denounce the high places; they were suppressed by Hezekiah and Josiah, and never restored after the Return.

iv. CITIES OF REFUGE. Num. xxxv.; Deut. xix; Josh. xx.—Of the six cities of refuge, Kedesh-Naphtali and Hebron were certainly ancient sanctuaries, and probably all were seats of important high places, so that the right of asylum assigned to them, was an ancient privilege retained when the sanctuaries were suppressed.

v. TABERNACLE AND TEMPLE.—In view of the historical continuity of the Tabernacle and the Temple we may consider these as a single institution, which attained its ideal status and full significance in the position accorded to the Temple at the close of the Monarchy and after the Captivity. It was—

(a) *Unique.* Deut. xii.; Lev. xvii.—In this advanced state of Jewish religion, the Temple became, not merely the typical Israelite sanctuary, the only one recognised as fully legitimate, but practically the sole sanctuary of Jehovah. The synagogues (see below) stood on an entirely different footing; and the existence of the Samaritan Temple and the Egyptian Temple built by the High Priest Onias never seriously affected the position of the Temple at Jerusalem. The multitude of the high places tended to polytheism; the "God of Bethel" might easily be thought of as a different deity from the "God of Beersheba," just as "Our Lady of Loretto" is distinguished from "Our Lady of Lourdes." But the exclusive reverence paid to the Temple at Jerusalem emphasised the Divine Unity; the one sanctuary implied One God.

(b) *Graduated Sanctity.* Lev. xvi.; Ezek. xlii., xlvi. —Though all Palestine was sacred, the presence of the Temple and the association with David and his dynasty made Jerusalem a sacred city—*i.e.*, possessing a sanctity a degree higher than that of the country generally; and the Temple, again, possessed a still higher degree of sanctity. But in the Temple itself the different courts and chambers possessed a graduated sanctity. The courts were open to the people, the outer and larger chamber was opened to the priests for their ordinary ministrations at the golden candlestick, the table of shew-bread, and the altar of incense, and was called "the Sacred Place." But, as in most ancient Temples, there was a small innermost chamber. Here Jehovah's presence was most specially manifested, and was symbolised by the presence—and later on by the memory of the presence—of the ark, the most sacred object of Israelite religion. This chamber was called Qodesh haq-Qodashim, "The Most Sacred Place" (R.V., "Holy of Holies"), and was entered by the High Priest alone, and only on one day in the year.

vi. SYNAGOGUES.—After the Return, the need for local sanctuaries, once supplied by the high places, was met by the institution of synagogues, where God was worshipped by prayer and praise, without sacrifice.

19. Sacred Persons. i. THE NATION.—In Exod. xix. 5, 6, Jehovah promises that, if Israel " will obey My voice indeed, and keep My covenant, then ye shall be a peculiar treasure unto Me from among all peoples ... a kingdom of priests and a sacred nation"—*i.e.*, Israel was a nation to whom Jehovah was manifested, the object of His special Providence, the people set apart to obey and worship Him in that most acceptable way which was made known by the prophets and the law. The various terms— divine election, sovereignty, fatherhood, marriage, protection, covenant (cf § 14)—which are used to express the mutual relation of Jehovah and Israel, all emphasise the sanctity of the chosen people.

The sanctity of the nation necessarily included all its tribes, clans, families, and individuals, and even extended in some measure to resident aliens and slaves of foreign birth. Hence the whole civil life of the nation, on its social, and especially on its family side, the mutual claims and duties of all its members, are the subject of divine revelation. Civil law and social custom are alike supported by religious sanctions, and each man's life is hedged about with ceremonial observances and regulations so that it almost becomes a continuous ritual.

ii. THE ROYAL DYNASTY AND THE KING.—As Jehovah had chosen Israel out of the nations, so He chose David and his house to be the rulers of His people. The election of the dynasty implies the principle of hereditary succession.

The legislation, however—in the form in which it has been preserved for us—dates from the Restoration, when the highest civil authority was the representative of Persia, and—apart from this Persian governor—the High Priest was the civil, as well as the ecclesiastical, head of the Jews. The law, therefore, has little to say about the king; Deut. xvii. 14-20, simply provides that the king shall be the Elect of Jehovah and an Israelite, that he shall make a copy of the law, study it diligently and observe it faithfully. Hence O. T. teaching with regard to the king is chiefly to be sought in the prophetical and historical books. As Judges, Samuel, Kings, and the earlier prophets do not apply the term "sacred" either to kings or priests, we are left to deduce the sanctity of the king from his functions. We may, however, note that Lev. iv. 3-16 implies the supreme sanctity of the ancient king, by transferring his title "Anointed," *mashiaḥ*, to the High Priest.

The king was, in a sense, sacred as the head and civil ruler of the sacred nation. But the king is sacred, in a more special and technical sense, as the religious head of the nation; and in this capacity he partakes of the character both of priest and prophet.

As Deuteronomy suggests, we find the royal authority resting on divine choice, confirmed by popular consent. This authority is supreme —under Jehovah—in all matters, civil and religious. The movements and housing of the ark, the building and repair of the Temple, the celebration of feasts are originated and controlled, not by the priesthood but by the kings, David, Solomon, Joash, Hezekiah, and Josiah. The original founder of the Law and the other religious institutions of Israel is not Aaron the Priest, but Moses "the king in Jeshurun" (Deut. xxxiii. 5), to whom Aaron is in all things subordinate. In prophetic fashion, the king receives direct communications from Jehovah—*e.g.*, Solomon's dream; and, like a priest, he sacrifices—*e.g.*, David (2 Sam. xxiv. 25), Solomon (1 Kings iii. 4); offers public prayers—*e.g.*, Solomon (1 Kings viii.); reads the Law to the people—*e.g.*, Josiah (2 Kings xxiii. 2).

The position of the "prince" in Ezek. xliv.-xlvi. corresponds in essential points to that of the actual kings of Judah. He is supreme "in his own sphere," and "it must not be supposed that . . . his authority is overshadowed by that of a priestly caste."* The prince is the religious representative of the nation as supplying the materials for public sacrifice (xlv. 17), and as possessing special rights of access to the sanctuary (xliv. 1-3). At the same time Ezekiel, by implication, excludes the prince from sacrifice and

* Skinner's *Ezekiel*, 147.

other priestly functions. The chronicler's explanation of Uzziah's leprosy as a punishment for exercising the priestly function of offering incense in the Temple, shows the same tendency. Otherwise Chronicles depicts the kings as almost more supreme in ecclesiastical affairs than they appear in Kings.

Accordingly the king and the monarchy are regarded as divine gifts to Israel, special tokens of Jehovah's favour; "the shout of a king" in Israel is a sign of the divine presence (Num. xxiii. 21; cf. xxiv. 7). On the other hand, the unfortunate experiences of the closing periods of both Israelite kingdoms weakened for a time the Jewish reverence for the monarchy, and an anti-monarchical sentiment finds expression in 1 Sam. viii. 12 (possibly referred to in Hosea ix. 9), and more moderately in Deut. xvii. 14-20.

iii. LEVITES (Num. i. 8, 18; Ezek. xliv. 9-14).— Out of the sacred nation, the tribe of Levi are elect of God, and invested with a special sanctity to perform the less important priestly functions of the Temple. Their service, as a substitution for the offering of the firstborn in sacrifice, represents the dedication of Israel to Jehovah.

iv. PRIESTS (Lev., Num., Ezek. xliv. 15, 16).—Out of this sacred tribe, the clan of Aaron—styled in Ezek. "the Levitical priests, of the house of Zadok"— are invested with a still higher sanctity. They are the priests of Israel, the higher functions of worship are their exclusive privilege, and they alone may enter the Sacred Place.

v. THE HIGH PRIEST (Exod. xxviii., xxix.; Lev.

viii., ix.).—Finally a priestly dynasty is chosen out of the sacred clan. The legal representative of this sacred dynasty is the hereditary head of the priesthood, the High Priest. The highest functions of public worship are exclusively reserved to him and he alone enters the Most Sacred Place. Speaking generally, the principles of heredity and primogeniture are thus recognised for the high-priesthood as well as for the monarchy—*e.g.*, Aaron is succeeded by his eldest surviving son, and similarly Eleazar by his son Phinehas. In practice, however, this theory of the law only represents the normal arrangement, the direct heirs being sometimes set aside. Throughout the history instances occur in which the priesthood was transferred from one family to another by the civil ruler, acting with or without divine sanction —*e.g.*, the deposition of Abiathar by Solomon (1 Kings ii. 26, 27).

vi. GRADUATED SANCTITY.—The principle of graduated sanctity is first illustrated by the gradual election of Israel; Seth is chosen from among the sons of Adam; Noah from among the Sethites; Shem from among the sons of Noah; Abraham from among the the sons of Shem; Isaac from among the sons of Abraham; and finally Israel from among the sons of Isaac. Thus Israel is the purest grain left after the repeated sifting of the nations. But, as we have seen, the graduation continues within Israel and ascends through the Levites and the house of Aaron to its climax in the supreme sanctity of the High Priest.

vii. REPRESENTATION OF ISRAEL TO JEHOVAH.—We

have seen above (§ 16, vi.) that kings and priests, in some measure, represented Jehovah to Israel. On the other hand the king by his provision of buildings and sacrifices for public worship, and in all his public acts that looked Godward, also represented his people before Jehovah. But this representation was more peculiarly the characteristic function of the priest. The king was obviously unsuited to be the ordinary mediator between Jehovah and Israel in the sphere of ritual. The constant observance of the multifarious details of ancient ritual would have have made far too great demands on his time. Moreover, the special degree of sanctity demanded from the ministrants in sacred ritual involved niceties of etiquette, dress, and diet incompatible with the exigencies of practical life. Accordingly the priests, in their various orders of Levite, Priests, and High Priests were set apart to represent Israel before Jehovah; by their pure descent, their physical perfection, their honourable marriage, their exceptional degree of ceremonial cleanness (Lev. xxi.), they were qualified to represent the nation in the performance of the most solemn ritual, and, in the person of the High Priest, to carry the confessions, prayers, thanksgivings, and offerings of the people into the Most Sacred Place, which symbolised the presence chamber of Jehovah.

viii. PROPHETS.—The prophet, as we have already seen, is mainly Jehovah's messenger to Israel. His divine commission, however, would naturally confer a certain sanctity; and, indeed, Elisha is called "a holy man of God" (2 Kings iv. 9), yet in the strictest sense, he is not "sacred"—*i.e.*, he has no special connection with the ritual by which Israel expressed its devotion to Jehovah; He is not set apart by Israel as its representative in religious matters.

Consequently the qualifications of the prophet contrast, at almost every point, with those of the priest. The latter must belong to a certain tribe or clan, the High Priest must—in theory—be in the direct line of male succession from Aaron; the prophet may be of any tribe or family. The priest must possess physical qualifications, and is limited in the choice of a wife; neither set of rules applies to the prophet. The priest holds office in virtue of his birthright, by which he shares the family inheritance of a divine election made centuries before his time; the prophet derives his authority solely from a personal call, which he himself has experienced.

ix. SEERS, SONS OF THE PROPHETS (1 Sam. ix., x.; 1 Kings xviii.; 2 Kings ii.-vi.; Jer. xxvii., etc.; Ezek. xiii., etc.; Zech. xiii. 2-6).—O. T. draws a sharp distinction between the professional and the inspired prophet. The true prophetic status was entirely independent of any connection with a recognised order and could not be acquired by any such connection (Amos vii. 14). Nevertheless there was a prophetic order, with a regular professional status; and as the inspired prophet might often arise within this order or identify himself with it, the popular mind would often fail to distinguish him from the ordinary ecclesiastic. The professional order was numerous: we read of eight hundred and fifty prophets collected to meet Elijah at Carmel, and of a hundred prophets of Jehovah hidden by Obadiah (cf. also the other references above).

Their functions were similar to those of the inspired prophets; they were teachers and preachers, and claimed to receive revelations by dreams and visions. In 1 Sam. ix., x., the prophets are possessed by a kind of ecstasy. According to 1 Sam. ix. 9, these ancient prophets were called "seers," possibly because they exercised a kind of second sight. From 1 Sam. ix. we gather that people resorted to the seer to obtain supernatural information as to such very practical details as lost asses, and that they paid for this information. In later times this prophetic function degenerated into mere divination and magic. The members of the prophetic order apparently lived by their profession; in addition to the above instance, we read that four hundred prophets of Baal ate at Jezebel's table, and doubtless pious princes were not less liberal to prophets of Jehovah. We are not expressly told how a man entered this prophetic order; probably, as is implied in the case of Saul, a capacity for ecstasy was one qualification; also, a man might be acknowledged as a prophet when he claimed, like Isaiah and Jeremiah, to have received a divine call; moreover, the history of Elisha shows that the prophet sometimes received his call from another prophet, whose disciple and assistant he became. Women also, like Deborah, might be prophetesses. The common theory that the prophetic guilds, "sons of the prophets," were devoted to the study of religious tradition and literature is, at any rate, a very plausible one. In the earlier history, Samuel, Elijah, and Elisha are closely identified with the prophetic order; but later on Jeremiah, Ezekiel, and the author of Zech. xii.-xiv., denounce the prophets as seeking, in the interests of tradition, to hinder men from accepting new truths of divine revelation. The Levitical law and the legal edition of the history —Chronicles—ignore the professional prophets.

x. THE REMNANT, § 6, vii.—The prophetic doctrine of the Remnant recognises a new community of faithful Israelites gathered out of unfaithful Israel.

xi. NAZIRITES (Num. vi.) appear in the Law as consecrated in a special way, by a temporary vow to abstain from intoxicants and from cutting of the hair. The instances in history, Samuel and Samson, were under a vow for life.

xii. SCRIBES (Ezra vii. 6, 21, 25).—In the period of later Judaism, when written records were superseding the immediate guidance of the Divine Spirit, the scribes, or students and interpreters of these records and especially of the law, in some measure took the place of prophetic teaching. Ezra is their prototype,* and his reformation is the first evidence that supreme religious influence had passed from the prophets and priests to the scribes.

20. Sacred Seasons. i. SANCTITY OF ALL TIME.— As the sacred places and persons represented the sanctity of the land and the nation, so modern thought may regard the sacred seasons as representing the sanctity of all time. But this idea is too abstract to be formulated in O. T. Nevertheless, when we examine the sacred seasons in detail, we shall see that they have reference to all seasons. As the land is God's permanent provision for the

* The "scribes" in Samuel and Kings are state secretaries.

physical needs of Israel, so the processes of the seasons, rain, heat, and cold, and the natural forces of vegetation, are His continuous working, through which the land yields its increase. The same necessity which led to the setting apart of sacred places and persons, also led to the consecration of special seasons. The sanctity of nature became more conspicuous by such concentration, and it was then possible to bring the whole people to the sacred places—the high places or the temple—and to permit them to witness the ministrations of their sacred representatives—the priests.

ii. THE AGRICULTURAL FEASTS.—The elaborate and somewhat artificial gradation in the sanctity of the soil and the nation, is only partly paralleled in that of the seasons. The natural sequences of the year were too imperious to be ignored in the interests of ritual symmetry. Hence we are concerned with the agricultural calendar. Immediately before the barley harvest—which precedes the wheat harvest —was held the Feast of Unleavened Bread (*Maççoth*), at which the firstfruits of the barley harvest were presented to Jehovah (Lev. xxiii. 10-12). After an interval of seven weeks, occupied by the wheat harvest, came the harvest feast (Exod. xxiii. 16), at which were offered the firstfruits of the wheat (Lev. xxiii. 15-17), and of all the products of the soil (Exod. xxiii. 19 ; Deut. xxvi. 2, 10). The times of these feasts were obviously fixed by the practical needs of agriculture, and the whole harvest was consecrated by offering the firstfruits.

At the close of the vintage, came the vintage

feast, the Feast of Ingathering (Exod. xxiii. 19), or Tabernacles (Lev. xxiii. 24; Deut. xvi. 13), at which firstfruits of wine and oil were offered. These were the three great feasts (Exod. xxiii. 14; Deut. xvi. 16), at which all males were to appear before Jehovah—*i.e.*, at His sanctuary. They linked the agricultural seasons into a sacred cycle, and recognised the fruits of the earth as Jehovah's gift to Israel.

iii. HISTORICAL FEASTS.—The three agricultural feasts recognised the sanctity of nature, and acknowledged Jehovah as the God of nature. So the historical feasts, by attaching a religious significance to the events of the national history, recognised Jehovah's moral government of the world, and saw the workings of His Providence therein. Motives of convenience would fix the commemoration of national anniversaries at the times of the agricultural feasts; even when such association was not determined by synchronism.

(*a*) *Passover* was celebrated in connection with the Feast of Unleavened Bread. Its ritual commemorated, in dramatic fashion, the slaying of the Egyptian firstborn and the exemption of the Israelites on the eve of the Exodus.

(*b*) *The Feast of Weeks* (*Pentecost*) is the name given in Deut. xvi. 10, to the harvest feast, where also the law of its observance contains the command: "Thou shalt remember thou wast a bondman in Egypt." Later Judaism gave a further historical significance to this feast by regarding it as the celebration of the giving of the law.

(c) *Tabernacles.*—The vintage feast came to be called the Feast of Tabernacles, because camping out in booths was regarded as a commemoration of the life in the wilderness. As the mode of life in the wilderness was not connected with any season of the year, this association with the vintage feast is clearly a mere matter of convenience.

(d) *Purim* (Esth. ix. 20-32) commemorated the deliverance of the Jews through Esther and Mordecai.

(e) *Dedication* commemorated the rededication of the Temple by Judas Maccabæus after its profanation by Antiochus Epiphanes.

(f) *Fasts* (Zech. vii. 3-5, viii. 19).—The disasters of the close of the Jewish monarchy were commemorated during the exile by fasts.

iv. ASTRONOMICAL FEASTS.—The agricultural feasts, as dependent on the annual circuit of the sun, are in a sense astronomical, but their significance connects with the ripening of grain and fruit, and not with the movements of the heavenly bodies. Similarly the fixing of Passover and Tabernacles at a full moon was probably a matter of convenience. Some of the feasts, however, are distinctly astronomical, and imply the dominion of Jehovah over the heavens.

(a) *New Moon.*—This is the sacred season most frequently referred to in the history and the prophets. Little stress is laid upon it in the legislation—cf., however, Ezekiel and Chronicles—probably because its observance was associated with the corruptions of the high places.

(b) *New Year, Feast of Trumpets* (Lev. xxiii. 24, 25), was a special case of the new moon.*

(c) *Sabbath*, in its widest sense, is a term applied to any sacred season, as one of rest, but its special and most usual meaning is the concluding day of a week of seven days. The time of observance of the sabbath of course depended on the apparent movements of the sun—*i.e.*, the succession of days and nights, but the period of seven days probably corresponds to a quarter of a lunar month (29½ days), either as a rough approximation, or because originally a day or two were set apart for the festival of the new moon. According to Gen. i.-ii. 4a, the six working days correspond to the period occupied by God in creating the Universe, and the sabbath to the period during which God rests after having finished His Creation. Thus man's labour and rest symbolise and commemorate the divine activity and the divine repose. In Deut. v. 15 the sabbath is regarded as a commemoration of the Exodus.

(d) *Seven as a Sacred Number.*—A week, or period of seven days, being thus definitely marked off by the constantly recurring observance of the sabbath, the periods of the Jewish calendar are naturally reckoned by weeks. Passover and Tabernacles each last a week, though in the Levitical law an extra day is added. Then by analogy "seven" is treated as a sacred number for other periods than days, and for other objects than periods. Thus the Feast of

---

* This "New Year" was the civil year, and was the middle —1st of 7th month—of the sacred year, which began with Nisan, about Easter.

Weeks, is seven—or a week of—weeks after Passover; the sabbatical year, when the land rests, came every seventh year; and the Jubilee at the close of seven times seven years. These periods of cessation from labour are not merely humane and utilitarian; at such times, Israel, the people, the land, and all living creatures, is stilled into silent reverence before Jehovah.

v. THE DAY OF ATONEMENT (Exod. xxx. 10; Lev. xvi., xxiii. 26-32; Num. xxix. 7-11. Cf. Ezek. xlv. 18-20).—This great fast day stands apart from all other sacred seasons; it does not connect with agriculture, national history, or the lunar or solar calendar. It is apparently fixed for the 10th day of the 7th month with reference to Tabernacles on the 15th. Its ritual symbolised the purification of the Most Sacred Place, the Temple, the altar, the priesthood, the nation, and the land from all uncleanness contracted during the previous year. It was thus a necessary preparation for the great rejoicings of Tabernacles, the most popular of O. T. feasts, at which the whole produce of the sacred soil and of the labours of the sacred nation was consecrated to Jehovah. The purification of the Day of Atonement assured the people that their offerings would not be rendered unacceptable by any taint of uncleanness, and that they might safely enjoy the fruits of the earth. According to the correct reading—cf. LXX. and R.V.Mg.—Ezekiel proposed to establish a day of atonement to be observed every six months.

21. Sacred Acts. i. IN CONNECTION WITH THE LAND.—The ritual observances of Israel, its religious acts and abstentions, are naturally connected with the sanctity of nature and of the land, of Providence and the nation. The sanctity of the land is symbolised by abstention from cultivation during the sabbatical and Jubilee years, by various regulations intended to secure the ceremonial cleanness of the land—*e.g.*, against sowing mingled seed (Lev. xix. 19), for the expiation of crime by an unknown hand (Deut. xxi. 1-9), by the offering of firstfruits and firstlings, and by sacrifices of thankoffering. Moreover, land and people were alike included in the more general observances of the national ritual.

ii. IN CONNECTION WITH THE PEOPLE. (*a*) *Circumcision* (Gen. xvii.; Lev. xii. 3).—The physical mark of circumcision was an outward token of the consecration of Israel to Jehovah; as a national observance and one of the conditions of the covenant between Jehovah and Israel, it was obligatory on male Israelites and on all foreigners admitted to the Passover (Exod. xii. 48). In Deut. x. 16, xxx. 6, and Jer. iv. 4, the rite of circumcision is used as a figure for spiritual purification.

(*b*) *Cleanness* (Lev. v.-xv.; Num. xix.; Deut. xiv. Cf. Haggai ii. 10-14).—As a rule, cleanness is the indispensable external condition of sanctity in things and persons. Cleanness is also required of every one and every thing brought into contact with sacred things and persons. Cleanness in persons consists in the state of body—*e.g.*, issues, menstruation, leprosy, childbirth, etc., render unclean—and in the use of proper food. Moreover, uncleanness—not cleanness—is contagious, both things and persons become unclean through contact with persons, animals, and things already unclean. All dead bodies, certain animals, etc., were unclean in themselves and communicated uncleanness.

In the more advanced stages of Israelite religion, the uncleanness of certain definite persons, animals, things in themselves, or in certain states, or under certain conditions, had become a matter of established custom, the original ground of their uncleanness was unknown, and O. T. takes the customs for granted, without feeling that they needed to be justified. But the cleanness of the Law included the avoidance of everything mean and filthy, as unworthy of a people consecrated to Jehovah, and as disqualifying from enjoyment of the sacred land, and from participation in the national fellowship with Jehovah.

(c) *War*.—In ancient Israel, victory in battle was regarded as a most important form of Jehovah's favour for His people. Accordingly Micah (iii. 5, etc.) speaks of "hallowing" or "consecrating"—*i.e.*, declaring war.

(d) *Sacrifices* were of very varied and general significance and will be dealt with separately below. They often served to express the sanctity of Israel, either as tokens of devotion to Jehovah, or as the ritual prescribed to remove ceremonial uncleanness.

(e) *Other Rites*.—Washings, sprinkling with blood or ashes, were also prescribed as a means of purification.

iii. CONNECTION OF SACRED ACTS WITH THE SANCTUARIES, FEASTS, AND PRIESTHOOD. — Sacrifices, the ordinary act of Israelite worship, according to the

Levitical law could only be offered at the Temple, with the aid of the priests, and were most numerous and important at the feasts and fasts. There was thus a kind of mutual sanctification, the sacrifices secured and increased the sanctity of the feasts and fasts, the Temple, and the priesthood; and the sacrifices themselves obtained a greater sanctity from the places and seasons at which they were offered and the persons who assisted at the celebration. The ordinary custom of the monarchy was not that prescribed by the Levitical law; popular usage recognised numerous sanctuaries which were doubtless the usual places for offering sacrifices, but altars were erected in many other places, and sacrifices frequently offered, without any professional assistance.

iv. SACRIFICES. (*a*) *Occasion.*—These were the ordinary and necessary acts of Israelite, as of almost all ancient religions. The term is often extended to include any and every kind of offering to the Deity. As the motives and circumstances of such gifts are very varied, the significance and character of sacrifices were equally varied. They were offered on almost every occasion of religious worship, at the daily morning and evening service of the Temple, on the sabbaths, new moons, and other feasts; on all special religious occasions, especially by way of thanksgiving at the consecration of the Tabernacle and the Temple, and of Nehemiah's walls, and at the installation of the ark in Zion; at the ordination of priests, at the conclusion of the covenants (Exod. xxiv. 5; Psalm l. 5, etc.), on occasions of public danger—*e.g.*, before the battle of Ebenezer (1 Sam. vii. 9); for the cleansing of

ISRAEL AS PEOPLE OF JEHOVAH

leprosy, the trial of jealousy (Num. v. 18), on the renewal or fulfilment of a Nazirite vow (Num. vi.), or in connection with the cleansing of individuals, officials, or the nation from accidental breaches of the law, and from some other forms of wrongdoing. Sacrifices, however, are not offered in atonement for wilful, heinous sins.

(b) *Bloodless Offerings.*—To define sacrifice as any offering is accurate from certain points of view, yet it imperfectly corresponds to either O. T. or English usage. Except *qorban*, which is a technical term confined to the Levitical law, O. T. has no word, in common use, which covers so wide an area of meaning, but makes a broad distinction between bloodless and animal offerings. Popular English uses "sacrifice" of animal offerings. Before considering these, however, we must notice the various kinds of bloodless offerings. All gifts for the Temple and the priesthood were regarded as offerings to Jehovah. The most common term for such offerings is *teruma*, "heave-offering," Temple tribute (Exod. xxx. 13), land (Ezek. xlv. 1), tithes (Num. xviii. 26), contributions for the construction of the Tabernacle (Exod. xxv. 2), portions of sacrifices given to priests—*e.g.* "heave-shoulder" (Lev. vii.). A less common term is *tenupha*, "wave-offering"; it is similar in etymological meaning and in application to *teruma*; the "wave-breast" (Lev. vii. 31), and "wave-sheaf," etc. (Lev. xxiii.), were portions given to the priests, and the gold offered for the Tabernacle (Exod. xxxviii. 24) is called *tenupha*. Both terms were apparently derived from the manner of presentation before Jehovah.

While *teruma* and *tenupha* were general terms, which might include part of an animal sacrifice, *minḥa* (A.V., "meat-offering," R.V., "meal-offering"), in the legislation,* becomes a technical term for an offering of meal or some form of corn, mixed with oil, frankincense, and salt (Lev. ii., vi., 14-18; Num. xv. 1-16). Special forms of the *minḥa* were the *minḥa qena'oth*, "offering of jealousy," in the ritual observed when a wife was suspected of adultery (Num. v. 15), and the *minḥa* of the *'asham* (A.V., "trespass-offering," R.V., "guilt-offering," Lev. v. 11); no oil or frankincense were mixed with these *minḥas*. The "drink-offering," *nesek*, consisted of wine (Num. xv. 1-16). The *minḥa* and *nesek* were the usual accompaniments of the ordinary animal sacrifices, but they were also offered independently.

In addition to the use of frankincense with the *minḥa*, incense was burnt on the altar of incense, and in the Most Sacred Place on the Day of Atonement. Exod. xxx. 3-38 gives a recipe for "most sacred" incense. It is apparently intended that this special incense was to be exclusively used for the altar of incense and the ritual of the Day of Atonement.

Another special bloodless offering was the "shewbread," *leḥem* (*hap*) *panim*, bread of the face or presence, (*leḥem*) *ma'areketh*, bread laid in order (Lev. xxiv. 5-9; cf. Exod. xxv. 30, xxxv. 13; 1 Sam. xxi. 1-7). Twelve loaves, sprinkled like the *minḥa* with frankincense—*lebona*, apparently not the "most sacred" incense—were placed on the table of

* In earlier literature it is almost a synonym for the later *qorban*.

shewbread in the Sacred Place, every sabbath at the end of the week they were eaten by the priests in a sacred place. They are, nevertheless, said to be "most sacred . . . amongst the fire-offerings of Jehovah," the reference probably being to the incense. The mention in Exod. xxv. 29, xxxvii. 16 ; Num. iv. 7, of bowls, flagons, and spoons, for the table of shewbread, has been held to indicate that drink-offerings were offered with the shewbread.*

(c) *Animal Sacrifices.*—*Zebah*—of which "sacrifice" in E.V., is usually the equivalent—meant originally a slaughter. The etymology suggests "sacrifice" as a religious function invariably connected with any meal at which flesh was eaten, or more accurately, as the religious aspect of such a feast. It was not a mere grace before or after meat, the whole meal was sacramental. By the burning of certain parts of the festal ox or sheep, Jehovah received a share of the meal and the feast became a symbol of His fellowship with His worshippers. The dominant interest in such a sacrifice was only religious, in the sense in which all ancient life was religious. Such sacrifices symbolised the sanctity of the enjoyment of temporal blessings; cf. the sacrificial feast to which Samuel invited Saul, and the annual sacrifice of David's family at Bethlehem.

In view of the etymology of *zebah*, and of the fact that *zbh* is used—though not exclusively—for offering all kinds of animal sacrifices, and that altars used for all such sacrifices are *mizbeahs*, we should expect to find *zebah* as a general term for all

* Schultz, i. 355.

kinds of animal sacrifices; but such a use of *zebaḥ* is rare. Even from the beginning a sharp distinction is made between the sacrificial feast, at which Jehovah and His people united in one common gladness, and the sacrifices offered as a means of sanctification, purification and expiation. The constant association of *zebaḥ* with the feast practically limited its use to those sacrifices of the later ritual, which retained most of the old festal sense of joyous fellowship with Jehovah. Accordingly *zebaḥ, zebaḥ shelamim, shelamim* (as plural; the sing. only Amos v. 22), E.V., "peace offering," R.V. Mg., "thank-offering," are usually equivalent terms. The word *shelamim* connects with the root *sh l m*, to requite, or repay. It represented the gratitude and devotion to Jehovah, naturally felt at any festal meal; it is therefore associated with the national feasts, both ordinary and special, and also expressed individual gratitude for special mercies. The *z. sh.* might be the fulfilment of a vow, a freewill offering, *nedaba*, or a sacrifice of thanksgiving *z. toda*, or *z. teru'a* (Psalm xxvii. 6). The *z. sh.* is sharply distinguished from the *'ola* (E.V., "burnt offering"), by the fact that only *part* of it—mostly the fat—was consumed on the altar, and the rest was eaten by the offerers and by the priests. In these, as in all sacrifices, the victim was to be without blemish, and the offerer laid his hand on the head of the victim, and its blood was sprinkled on the altar (Lev. iii., vi. 12; vii., xix. 5-8).

The *'ola*, E.V., "burnt-offering"—"that which goes up," either on to the altar or in smoke to heaven, is constantly coupled with *zebaḥ, z. sh., shelamim*, and in many cases each noun is governed by a cognate verb—*e.g.*, 1 Sam. vi. 15, *he'elu 'oloth wayyizbeḥu zebaḥim*, " they sent up *'olas* and slaughtered *zebaḥs*." The *'olas* and *zebaḥs* are thus indicated as the two great classes of sacrifices. The characteristic feature of the *'ola* was that the *whole* of the animal was burnt. Hence the symbolism was not that of fellowship, but of gift pure and simple, entire surrender. The rite became the natural expression of any intense feeling of gratitude, petition, or propitiation (Lev. i. 4), and formed, as it were, the natural basis of almost all acts of public and private worship.

The *ḥaṭṭath* (E.V., "sin-offering," Lev. iv., v., vi. 24-30; Num. xv. 22); and *'asham*, (A.V., "trespass offering," R.V., "guilt-offering," Lev. v.-vii., xiv., xix.; cf., for both, Ezek. xl.-xlvii.) are not clearly distinguished. In Lev. vii. 7 we read, "As is the *ḥaṭṭath* so is the *'asham*: there is one law for both," and according to Schultz (i. 380, note), " in Lev. v. 6-8, 12, *'asham* and *ḥaṭṭath* are interchanged, as absolutely synonymous." Both serve to remove uncleanness or loss of sanctity caused by sin, see for *ḥ.* Lev. iv. 1-3, and for *'a.* Lev. v. 1-6, vi. 1-7; and, as we have seen above, both are said to have the same ritual, etc. In view of the enumeration of offences in Lev. v. 1-vi. 7, for which an *'a.* must be offered as compared with the more general statements in iv. 1-3, with regard to the *ḥ*, it appears that *'a.* was to be offered in compensation for wrong done to the material rights of God or man, injury to property, or the withholding of what was lawfully due; *ḥ* was required to atone for any breach of Jehovah's commands. The directions as to ritual are in some passages practically identical for both—*e.g.*, Lev. iv. 28, 32, v. 6; but under *ḥ.* we have provisions for what is to be offered by an individual, by the congregation, by the ruler; under '*a.* by individuals of different degrees of wealth. A regulation peculiar to the '*a.* is that the wrongdoer is to make compensation to the full amount of his fraud, plus one-fifth. The ritual of *ḥ.* was as follows: the priest was to lay hands on the victim, kill it, sprinkle part of the blood before the veil, put some on the horns of the altar of incense, and pour out the rest at the base of the altar of burnt-offering. The fat was to be removed and burnt on this altar, and the rest to be burnt "without the camp, in a clean place, where the ashes were poured out." In the regulations for the '*a.*, however, the residue of the flesh was to be eaten by the priests in a sacred place (Lev. vii. 6; cf. v. 13). The poor man's '*a.* may take the form of a *minḥa* offered without oil or frankincense.

'*A.* occurs in 1 Sam. vi. and 2 Kings xii. 16, as a fine or money penalty; otherwise neither '*a.* nor *ḥ.* occurs in the history except in Chron., Ezra, Neh., or in the prophets except in Ezekiel. While *ḥ.* occurs frequently in the Levitical laws; '*a.* is only enjoined in cases of compensation, and in cleansing leprous persons or houses (Lev. xiv. 15), and in renewing Nazirite vows (Lev. vi. 12).

(*d*) *Grouping of Sacrifices.*—The *minḥa* and *nesek* might sometimes be offered alone—*e.g.* the *minḥa* for an '*asham* (Lev. vii.), David's *nesek*, (2 Sam. xxiii. 16),

ISRAEL AS PEOPLE OF JEHOVAH 151

but usually they were appendages of other sacrifices (cf. above). Since, when an 'asham consisted of a pair of birds, one of them was to be the 'asham and the other an 'ola, we may perhaps gather that an 'ola usually accompanied an 'asham or ḥaṭṭath. In the ritual of the Day of Atonement an 'ola accompanies the ḥaṭṭath; so also in Lev. xiv., xv.; Num. vi., vii., xxviii., xxix. In the history (Judges—2 Kings), 'ola and zebaḥ shelamim sometimes occur, each of them, alone; but much more frequently coupled together. The daily service of the Temple included the offering of two lambs, one in the morning, and one in the evening, as a "continual burnt-offering" ('olath tamid; Exod. xxix. 38-46); in the ritual of the New Moon, First Fruits, Passover, Trumpets, Day of Atonement, and Tabernacles, this is supplemented by other 'olas and combined with a ḥaṭṭath. In the account of the Dedication of the Tabernacle (Num. vii.), and in similar narratives in 2 Chron. xxix., xxxi., we have a complete set of sacrifices, 'ola, minḥa, zebaḥ, shelamim, ḥaṭṭath.

v. RITUAL OF PASSOVER (WITH FEAST OF UN-LEAVENED BREAD), Exod. xxiii. 15; Lev. xxiii. 5-8; Num. xxviii. 16-25; AND DAY OF ATONEMENT, Lev. xvi., xxiii. 26-32; Num. xxix. 7-11.—The characteristic features of the Passover (cf. above) were on the one hand the offering of firstfruits, on the other the dramatic commemoration of the events of the Exodus. On the Day of Atonement the High Priest, not in his special robes, but in the simple white linen garments of an ordinary priest, offered first a ḥaṭṭath and 'ola for himself and the whole priesthood; then he presented before Jehovah, at the door of the Temple two he-goats and a ram, and cast lots between the goats, that they might be assigned respectively to Jehovah and to Azazel. Then he offered the bullock as an 'ola and burnt incense and sprinkled the blood seven times before the ark, "to make atonement" (*kapper*) for himself and the priesthood. Then he similarly offered the goat assigned to Jehovah as a *ḥaṭṭath* for the Temple and the nation, and sprinkled its blood before the ark, and also sprinkled the blood of both victims on the altar of incense. Then he laid his hands on the goat assigned to Azazel (A.V., "the scapegoat," R.V., "the goat" . . . for Azazel), confessed over it the sins of the nation, and sent it away to be let loose in the wilderness, to "bear upon him all their iniquities unto a solitary land."

vi. OTHER FORMS OF WORSHIP.—A *vow* (Num. xxx.; Deut. xii., xxiii.) was a promise to make some offering or perform some service to Jehovah. It might be a simple expression of gratitude; but more often a vow, like Jacob's at Bethel, and like Jephthah's, was made on condition that Jehovah granted some favour. We have numerous examples of *prayer*—*e.g.*, Solomon's at the Dedication at the Temple, often followed by direct and prompt answer—*e.g.*, Samuel at Ebenezer. The granting of petitions is limited by the divine will—*e.g.*, Abraham's intercession for Sodom, and Jeremiah's for Judah, are rejected; and is conditioned by the sincerity of the worshipper (Psalm lxvi. 18). The Levitical law is silent as to prayer, but (Deut. xxvi. 1-11) provides a collect to be repeated by the offerer of firstfruits, which, however,

ISRAEL AS PEOPLE OF JEHOVAH 153

is a declaration rather than a petition. As regards *praise*, the history bears abundant testimony to the use of music, singing, and dancing to express thanksgiving, especially in connection with the ark and the Temple services. Although the legislation is again silent, the Psalter and the fact of its inclusion in the canon testify to the large part which was played by prayer and praise in the religious life of Israel.

vii. FASTS.—The only fast appointed by the Levitical law is that of the Day of Atonement. From Zech. vii. 5, viii. 19, we learn that the disasters of the close of the monarchy had been commemorated during the Captivity by fasts in the fourth, fifth, seventh, and tenth months, but that it was the will of Jehovah that these fasts should cease. Special fasts were also proclaimed on special occasions (Ezra viii. 21, etc.). There are no detailed regulations laid down for fasting: Lev. xxiii. 27, 29 simply describes it as "afflicting the soul," Isa. lviii. 5 speaks of the faster as "bowing down his head as a rush and spreading sackcloth and ashes under him." The essential feature of abstinence from food and drink was too familiar to need mentioning, and is everywhere taken for granted. The fast is a natural symbol of dejection caused by the sense of Jehovah's anger.

viii. DEDICATION OF PERSONS AND PLACES.—The setting apart of a person or place to a sacred office or use was accompanied by a complete set of sacrifices, etc., the significance of each being appropriate to such an occasion. The king, priest, or sanctuary needed to be cleansed from sin by the atoning rites of the *ḥaṭṭath*; such dedications were occasions for the gratitude and self-surrender of the *'ola*; they were marked instances of that fellowship with God and man expressed by the *zebaḥ shelamim*. The *z. sh.* is not distinctly specified in the ritual for ordination of priests in Exod. xxix., but the "ram of consecration" eaten by the priests in the sacred place is virtually a *z. sh.* The Levitical law, on account of the circumstances under which the extant edition was compiled, contains no ritual for a royal coronation, but 1 Sam. xi. 15; 1 Chron. xxix. 21, 22, mention the offering of numerous sacrifices on such occasions. The characteristic rite of such dedications was anointing with oil. We read of the anointing of Saul, Absalom, David, Solomon, Joash, Jehoahaz, and Jehu. It has been suggested that a king was only anointed under exceptional circumstances, when he founded a new dynasty, like David, or when his claim to the throne was disputed, like Solomon; but the use of the phrase "Jehovah's Anointed" as an ordinary royal title rather shows that all kings were anointed. For the anointing of the Tabernacle, altar, vessels, and priests, see Lev. viii. This anointing with oil is interpreted as a communication of the Spirit of Jehovah (cf. Zech. iv. 6).

The distinction between the status of the king or priest on the one hand, and the prophet on the other, is shown by the absence of any ritual dedication of the prophet. Elijah, apparently, is told (1 Kings xix. 16) to anoint his successor, but we are not told that he ever did so; and as Jehovah, in the same breath, bids him anoint two kings, the word "anoint" may only be applied to the successor in the prophetic office, in the loose general sense of appoint. There is no other reference to the anointing of a prophet; Isa. lxi. 1, "Jehovah hath anointed me to preach," etc., is, of course, figurative.

ix. BAN, *ḥerem*, A.V., "ACCURSED THING," R.V., "DEVOTED THING."—While sacrifices consisted of desirable and sacred materials which formed acceptable offerings, things evil and abominable were banned (A.V., "accursed," R.V., "devoted") by being utterly destroyed—*e.g.*, the inhabitants of heathen cities taken in war (Deut. xx. 10-18). The ban might extend to males only, or to all the inhabitants, and even to all living creatures. In the case of Jericho (Josh. x. 18) the ban extended to everything in the city, the indestructible metals being consecrated to Jehovah. Images of heathen gods are *ḥerem*. The ban, like uncleanness, is contagious, as in the case of Achan, and of the heathen images (Deut. vii. 26). In the above cases the ban is judicial and national, but individuals might ban; according to the analogy of the '*ola*, things which could not be sacrificed might be offered to Jehovah, by being destroyed as *ḥerem*, apparently even human beings (Lev. xxvii. 28, 29. Cf. the case of Jephthah's daughter). According to Num. xviii. 14, all *ḥerem*, like the silver and gold at Jericho, belongs to the priests, as Jehovah's representatives; and in Lev. xxvii. 28, *ḥerem* is said to be "most sacred," like the inner chamber of the Temple.

x. OATHS AND ADJURATIONS, BLESSINGS AND CURSES. —An Israelite used oaths—*i.e.*, invoked upon himself punishment from Jehovah—in case of falsehood or failure to keep faith, to attest his evidence, or clear his character (Exod. xxii. 6-11), or as a solemn form of promise to God or man. Such an appeal to Jehovah was a token of loyalty to Him and trust in Him (Deut. vi. 13). Similarly Eli adjures Samuel, in God's name, or, as we should say, for God's sake, to tell him the whole truth (1 Sam. iii. 17). Blessings and curses were solemn prayers for good or ill to fall upon the heads of others.

22. Sacred Objects. i. CLEAN AND UNCLEAN THINGS. —The sacred character of the nation and the land implied, in some measure, the sacred character of the objects contained in the land and familiarly used by the people. Hence in their normal state the belongings of an Israelite homestead should be clean.

On the other hand, as aliens and foreign lands had no sacred character, they and all belonging to them are, at any rate in some measure, unclean (Josh. xxii. 19; Hos. ix. 3). Moreover, human beings are also unclean in certain states and circumstances. Cf. § 21, ii. (b).

ii. THE APPARATUS OF WORSHIP.—In the strict sense, however, sacred objects were those connected with worship—the buildings erected for worship at the sacred places; the Temple, with its furniture, contents and belongings; and the dress and ornaments of the priests. The Temple (*hekal* = palace), was, as its name indicates, the palace of the Divine King of Israel. The Most Sacred Place is the royal presence chamber, where, on state occasions, He gives audience to the most distinguished of His subjects. The Sacred Place suggests a royal banqueting hall with its lamps and perfume of incense, and its table spread perpetually. The shewbread is, no doubt, from one point of view, a perpetual offering from Israel to Jehovah; but as the royal table would naturally be spread for guests, it may also symbolise Jehovah's continual bounty to Israel. The material of sacrifice is naturally sacred, and as it represents the different kinds of food, symbolises, like the firstfruits and firstlings, the consecration of cattle, grain, fruit, and their products and preparations. Special stress is laid upon the fat and the blood. The parts of the *zebaḥ* offered to Jehovah are chiefly the fat, probably because of their choiceness, possibly also because they would burn well. According to Lev. xvii. 11, etc., " The life of the flesh is in the blood: and I have given it you upon the altar to make atonement for your lives: for it is the blood that maketh atonement by reason of the life." The blood symbolised the most precious offering that could be made to Jehovah —the life of a living creature.

iii. THE ARK AND THE MERCY SEAT (Exod. xxv.-xl.; Lev. xvi.; Deut. x.).—In spite of the close connection between these two—the mercy seat covering the ark—they are described separately in the Pentateuch, and each plays its own part in the ritual.

The real importance of the ark, *'aron*—Noah's ark and the ark in the bulrushes are *teba*—belongs to the earlier pre-prophetic religion of Israel. It is referred to in the final form of O. T. religion as a venerable relic, long since lost. The tradition of its sanctity is still preserved and even serves to hallow the empty shrine, which replaces that in which the ark dwelt. It was above all else *the* symbol of the presence of Jehovah with Israel, and when it was lost this significance was transferred to the Most Sacred Place itself ; but neither in the history nor in the elaborate descriptions in the Pentateuch is any reason given why the ark symbolised the Divine Presence.

The ark was in the form of a sacred chest, such as is found in many religions, the closest parallel being the sacred boats of the Egyptians. Until the time of David it was borne in sacred processions, and especially was carried to battle to symbolise the presence of Jehovah Sabaoth, the Divine Ally of Israel. The only reference to the ark in the prophets is Jer. iii. 16: "When ye are multiplied and increased in the land, saith Jehovah, 'The ark of the Covenant of Jehovah' shall no longer be the watchword of Israel: men shall neither think of the ark nor remember it; they shall neither miss the ark nor make another in its place." Evidently the ark was lost, and the prophet desired that it might be consigned to oblivion.

In Deuteronomy and the Levitical law the special function of the ark is to contain the Tables of the covenant of Jehovah with Israel; thus suggesting that His most real presence with His people was to be found in the record of His moral revelation.

The name of the mercy seat—*kapporeth*—lends itself to two meanings. According to the original and literal meaning of the root *kpr*, it may mean

ISRAEL AS PEOPLE OF JEHOVAH 159

cover—*i.e.*, that which it actually was, the covering of the ark. According to the use of the verbal form *kipper*, to make atonement, it may mean place or means of atonement, referring to the fact that the mercy seat was only used in the ritual, in connection with the services of the Day of Atonement. Probably the literal meaning was the original, and the second meaning was attached to the name as the result of the place assigned to it in the ritual. As the Most Sacred Place is the royal audience chamber, so the mercy seat is the throne.

iv. MOST SACRED OBJECTS.—The description "most sacred"—*qodesh qodashim*—is given to the following: —the Tabernacle and its furniture (Exod. xxx. 22-29), the special incense, the shewbread, the *'asham*, the *ḥaṭṭath*, the priests' share of the *minḥa*, and the *ḥerem* (A.V., "accursed thing," R.V., "devoted thing"). The unique sanctity of the inner chamber of the sanctuary is marked by the use of the still more definite term *Qodesh-haq-Qodashim*.

23. The Sanctity of Israel.—Thus the Levitical law has an elaborate and complete theory of the sanctity of Israel, worked out with scientific precision. Doubtless it would be entirely symmetrical, but for the persistence of ancient customs too stubborn to be completely adjusted to a mathematical diagram. But we greatly wrong the law if we do not constantly bear in mind its moral presuppositions. The Pentateuch makes large provision for personal and social righteousness; and the ceremonial ordinances assume that the national life approximately corresponds to this high standard.

The sacred system of the Pentateuch may be compared to a pyramid, whose base is a pentagon, the five sides of which are the sacred people, the sacred land, the sanctity of time (sacred seasons), the sanctity of life (sacred acts), and the sanctity of matter (sacred objects). From these base lines, there is, in each case, a gradation to successively smaller classes, with a correspondingly increased sanctity, till the pyramid reaches its apex in the central rite of the Day of Atonement, the entry of the most sacred person, the High Priest, into the Most Sacred Place, on the most sacred day, and the performance of acts combining the most sacred acts and objects of the ritual, the offering of incense before the ark, and the sprinkling upon the mercy seat.

The conditions under which any such elaborate system could be even approximately carried out did not exist till the restoration; under the monarchy the religious life was far less symmetrical and much more simple and spontaneous. Moreover, the very mission of the prophets implied that they were indifferent or even hostile to ritual. The law itself assumes that national righteousness is a necessary antecedent to acceptable ritual; the prophets' work was to show that no such righteousness existed and to induce Israel to seek after it. Till their work was in some measure accomplished there could be no question of perfect ritual.

24. The Preservation and Renewal of Sanctity.—The Levitical theory of Israel is that the whole nation is sacred. Sin, even the sin of an individual, as in the case of Achan, destroys the sanctity of the nation and subjects it to the divine wrath. Hence, when sin has been committed the sanctity of the nation must be restored by putting away the sin. There is no forgiveness for heinous sins, in such cases the sanctity of the nation is restored by cutting off the offender from Israel, either by death (Achan) or by some unspecified mode of excommunication. The milder penalty was developed by later Judaism. The punishment of "cutting off" is threatened against the uncircumcised Israelite (Gen. xvii. 14), the man who eats leavened bread during the Passover (Exod. xii. 15, 19), the man who makes for profane purposes imitations of the sacred oil or incense (xxx. 33, 38), the sabbath-breaker (xxxi. 14), those who take part in sacred rites in a state of uncleanness, or eat blood or the part of a sacrifice which should be burnt on the altar (Lev. vii.), those who kill sacrificial animals or sacrifice elsewhere than at the central sanctuary (xvii.), those who are guilty of certain sexual offences (xviii., xx. 17, 18), or worship Moloch (xx. 1-6), or fail to observe the Day of Atonement (xxiii. 29), or the Passover (Num. ix. 13); the unclean person who fails to purify himself (xix. 13, 20), and generally any one who is guilty of "presumptuous" sin, sin "with a high hand" (*beyad rama*).

In the case of venial sins, the sanctity of the individual or the nation is restored by *ḥaṭṭath* or *'asham*. *Ḥaṭṭath* is prescribed for sins committed inadvertently (*bishegaga*, Lev. iv.; Num. xv. 22-29). *'Asham* is prescribed in similar cases, and also specially in case of any infringing or withholding of the rights of property of man or God (Lev. v.-vii.).

Thus the ritual, like O. T. generally, is concerned for "hidden sins" (Psalm xix. 12), sins of carelessness and omission committed inadvertently. The case of Achan illustrates a practical difficulty in the application of the principle—the author of some grievous sin might remain undiscovered. Achan was found out through the lot, but the law does not treat his case as a precedent. Deut. xxi. 1-9 provides a special rite to cleanse the land from the guilt of sins committed by some person or persons unknown. A heifer's neck was to be broken over running water, in a desolate valley. The elders of the nearest city were to wash their hands over it, in the presence of the priests, and to disclaim any knowledge of the crime and ask forgiveness for the nation. They were also to pray that Jehovah may not "suffer innocent blood to *remain* in the midst of Thy people Israel." As in Deut. xix. 13, "innocent blood" is "put away" from Israel by slaying the murderer, this last prayer is probably a petition that Jehovah will purge Israel of the guilt of this murder by Himself slaying the murderer.

But sacrifices could only be offered for specific sins of inadvertence, when the sinner had become aware of them; and many sins must have remained permanently "hidden" from the sinner. Moreover the very commission as well as the author of heinous crimes might remain unknown. Provision for the atonement for such sins is doubtless made in the *haṭṭaths* appointed for the various feasts; or individuals, as in Job i. 5, might offer sacrifices to atone for unknown sins; but the special atonement for sins, which had not been otherwise dealt with, was made on the Day of Atonement, when a *ḥaṭṭath* was offered to make "atonement for the sanctuary, because of the uncleanness of the Israelites, and because of their transgressions, *pesha'*, in all their sins, *ḥaṭṭath*, and the scapegoat carried away the iniquities, *'awon*, of Israel into the wilderness.

Here again the prophets dealt with a condition of things, in which there was no question of restoring the sanctity of Israel by atoning for venial sins and slaying or excommunicating grievous offenders. The whole nation was unclean. Nevertheless, the principle of cutting off offenders is applied to the whole nation, which is to be destroyed, and this destruction is to serve as a purification which may secure the sanctity of a New Israel in succeeding generations. Jehovah Himself purges away filth and guilt till every one left in Jerusalem is sacred (Isa. iv. 3, 4).

25. Doctrine of Sacrifice. — Questions naturally arise *first* as to how sacrifices served to secure the sanctity of Israel, and *second* as to what was the O. T. doctrine of sacrifice. We cannot wholly answer either of these questions. It would not be a gross exaggeration to say that the O. T. lays down no doctrine of sacrifice. Certain rites are commanded for given purposes, but the O. T. gives little or no reason for the rites, and states no theory of the ritual. The scriptural doctrine of sacrifice is mainly to be found in the N. T., and is, for the most part, either adapted from post-biblical Judaism or had its origin in the N. T. revelation; it therefore belongs chiefly to N. T. theology. We must, however, consider certain doctrines which the O. T. states or implies with regard to sacrifice.

(a) *Sacrifice not characteristic of the religion of Israel.*—Though sacrifice was appointed for Israel by divine revelation, it did not originate in this O. T. revelation. God took a universal and familiar rite and ordained it as a form of worship for His people. Many of the sacrifices and much of their connected ritual were similarly derived. O. T. betrays no consciousness that its sacrifices in their main external features, were essentially different from some of those offered by the heathen around. Deut. xxxii. 38 speaks of Israel offering *zebaḥ* and *nesek* to strange gods; in 2 Kings iii. 27, the king of Moab sacrifices a human *'ola*, and in v. 17 Naaman declares that he will offer *'ola* and *zebaḥ* to Jehovah alone. Hence, the original meaning and ground of much sacrificial ritual is antecedent to the Mosaic revelation.

(b) *Moral Conditions of Acceptable Sacrifice.*—The prophets and psalmists constantly repudiate the idea that sacrifices have any value apart from true moral and spiritual life. The language of the prophets does not mean that they denounced such observances; but whereas popular superstition regarded sacrifice as the most important of divine requirements, and as efficacious apart from the life and character of the offerer, the prophets assigned to sacrifice an entirely subordinate place in the religious life.

(c) *The Symbolism of Sacrifice.*—We have thus seen that a sacrifice, according to O. T revelation—as distinct from its original heathen sense and from the value constantly assigned to it by popular Jewish superstition—was a symbol and not an *opus operatum*; but we may ask, in the absence of any revealed O. T. interpretation, how far these symbols speak for themselves. Their meaning might be so obvious that we should be able to see at once how they must have been understood by devout Israelites. Such a hypothesis, however, is discredited by the many conflicting interpretations put forward with equal confidence. Hence, again, we must repeat—on the authority of N. T. itself, 1 Peter i. 10-12—that the N. T. interpretation of O. T. ordinances and teaching was not necessarily known to ancient Israel or part of O. T. revelation.

We may, however, indicate some of the more obvious suggestions of the symbolism of sacrifice.

i. The custom of the *zebaḥ shelamim* that the victim should be partly consumed on the altar, partly eaten by the priests, and partly by the offerer, symbolises friendly fellowship between Jehovah and His worshippers.

ii. All forms of sacrifice, being gifts or offerings, would naturally express gratitude to a benefactor; or obligation—by way of tribute—to a sovereign; or propitiation of an injured or offended lord.

iii. The death of the animal was necessarily involved in a feast upon its flesh, *zebaḥ shelamim*. In the case of other sacrifices, death was the most striking way in which the owner could at once part with his property and symbolise its reception by God. The blood, being regarded as the vehicle of the life, is reserved for Jehovah.

iv. Laying on of hands is common to all sacrifices

(*zebaḥ sh.*, Lev. iii. 2; *'ola*, Lev. i. 4; *ḥaṭṭath*, Lev. iv. 4, etc.; it is not mentioned in connection with the *'asham*, but is doubtless covered by Lev. vii. 7). It cannot, therefore, specially symbolise the atoning value of sacrifice, but rather the ownership of the animal by the offerer and his delivery of it to the priest as the representative of Jehovah.

v. The Ritual for Atonement.—To say that the main significance of all sacrifice was its virtue as atoning for sin would be an exaggeration, but yet the exaggeration of a truth. Any offering, whether as gift or tribute, was a natural expression of the sense of sin and the desire for reconciliation with God. Accordingly, it is said in Lev. i. 4 that the *'ola* shall be accepted to make atonement (cf. Ezek. xlv. 15-17). But the *ḥaṭṭath* and *'ola*, and the rites of the Day of Atonement, were specially appointed to reconcile the sinner to God. The features peculiar to this ritual and therefore specially symbolising the method and conditions by which God received the sinner to His mercy, are the sprinkling of blood before the veil and the placing of it on the horns of the altar of incense, and the burning of the greater part of the *ḥaṭṭath* without the camp (cf. iv. 46). The ritual of the Day of Atonement is, for the most part, a multiplication and expansion of these two acts. Special *ḥaṭṭaths* are offered, and the blood is sprinkled, not merely in the Sacred Place, but even upon the "mercy seat" in the Most Sacred Place. The other peculiar features of this day's ritual are that it is the only fast appointed by the law, and that beside the goat of the *ḥaṭṭath*, a goat "for Azazel" bears away the sins of the people into the wilderness.

The explanation of the sprinkling of the blood is given in Lev. xvii. 2, when the blood is said to "make atonement," *kapper*. The exact force of the term is matter of much controversy. *Kpr* means originally cover, and the atoning ritual is usually explained as covering sin, or the person or thing contaminated by sin or uncleanness, from the awful exposure to Jehovah's holiness* (Isa. vi.). Smend (p. 321), however, considers that *kpr* in the Levitical law does not refer back to the original sense of the root, but is formed afresh as a denominative from *kopher*, ransom or atoning payment. None of the explanations of *kapper* make it clear how the life of the victim avails to restore the Israelite to that normal state of sanctity in which he enjoys full religious privileges. A common explanation—derived from the N. T.—is that the death of the animal symbolises, and is accepted as a substitute for, the forfeited life of the sinner. However appropriate this view may be in the light of the N. T. history, and especially when sacrifices are considered as types of Christ's death, such an interpretation is nowhere explicitly furnished by O. T. itself, and is only suggested in Isa. liii. 10.

Lev. xvi. 21, 22 explains the burning of the *hattath* without the camp, and the driving away of the scapegoat, as symbolising the putting away of sin from within the bounds of Israel.

* Cave, *Scripture Doctrine of Sacrifice*, 514. Schultz, i. 398.

The meaning of "for Azazel" is one of the unsolved enigmas of O. T.; it has been variously explained as meaning "for sending away"; or the goat itself; or the place to which it was sent; or some evil spirit. It has been held to be a relic of pre-Mosaic ritual adopted into the Levitical law.*

In spite, however, of our ignorance as to the origin and primitive meaning of many details of the ritual, its broad and essential significance is clear. The atoning sacrifices express on the one hand man's sense of guilt, of the heinousness of sin, and on the other hand God's hatred of sin, His refusal to tolerate it, and, at the same time, His willingness to forgive the penitent. The special offering on the Day of Atonement of a sacrifice for Israel by the High Priest as the representative of the nation is recognised by N. T. as a type of the sacrifice made for the world by Christ as the representative of mankind.

vi. SACRIFICE AS A POSITIVE DIVINE ORDINANCE.— O. T. constantly states as the main reason for sacrifice and the guarantee of its efficacy, the fact that it is a divinely appointed means of grace. Sacrifices are to be offered because Jehovah had so commanded; they will obtain His favour and forgiveness because He had so promised.

* For details of various theories see Cave, 521.

CHAPTER VI

JEHOVAH AND THE ISRAELITE

CHAPTER VI

JEHOVAH AND THE ISRAELITE

26. The Nation and the Individual.—In considering O. T. teaching as to personal religion, we must always bear in mind that O. T. deals mainly with the nation, and, in most of its documents, approaches all questions from this standpoint. Even in Psalms which seem at first sight individualistic, the author is often identifying himself with his people. While the principles of righteousness, sin, retribution, and redemption are the same for a nation and an individual, the statement of doctrine in the two cases is very different. Many doctrines of national life can be applied to the individual with slight modification; in other cases the form of the doctrine must be wholly changed, and, in any case, the application requires great care.

For the most part the relation of the Israelite to Jehovah was mediated through Israel. Divine favour to Israel in the shape of fertility, prosperity and victory redounded to the advantage of the individual, and conversely the individual suffered under the chastisements inflicted upon Israel. But the correspondence of individual and national fortunes had many important exceptions, and by no means involved any invariable and exact punishment and reward of individual character and conduct. Israel might suffer for its sins and be rewarded for its virtue, but the righteous man suffered in the ruin of the nation and was not always blessed in its prosperity; while conversely the sinner might sometimes escape the one and would generally enjoy the other. The ultimate theory of national sanctity meets this difficulty by providing that the Israelite who fell into deadly sin should be cut off by death or expulsion, but this principle could never be fully applied in practice.

Moreover, as a rule, the religious life of the individual was mediated through the nation and its representatives. He worshipped through the priest or king; the national ritual of the Day of Atonement was the regular method by which he received assurance of reconciliation to God; his knowledge of the divine will came to him through the priest, the prophet, or the national tradition.

On the other hand the sanctity and righteousness of Israel were, so to speak, the integration of these virtues in the individual; and in theory the sanctity of Israel was annulled by a single individual sin, as in the case of Achan. Hence national righteousness is only partly manifested in the public ritual; it is for the most part built up out of the righteous lives of individuals; and we have now to consider in what this righteousness consisted, and how it was maintained and restored. For illustrations of personal religion we naturally have to look, for the most part, to the national leaders, judges, kings, and prophets; because history is mainly occupied with such characters. The priests are seldom personally conspicuous; the individual is lost in the office.

27. Individual Righteousness consisted in obedience to the revealed will of God, as expressed in legal ordinances and prophetic exhortations. These authorities covered the whole religious, personal, and social life of the Israelite. They enjoined the worship of Jehovah according to the pure ritual of the law, and abstention from the worship of other gods, or from unauthorised modes of worshipping Jehovah. They inculcated personal cleanliness and purity, and a careful respect for the rights of others, especially of parents and kinsfolk. Moreover, apart from legal and family claims, the Israelite is commanded to help the poor and any who are in distress. It is sinful to neglect an opportunity of saving even an enemy from accidental loss: "If thou meet thine enemy's ox or ass going astray, thou shalt surely bring it back to him again" (Exod. xxiii. 4). The law shows a certain care for the interests of foreigners, and even of dumb animals; and if the standard of conduct towards slaves, women, and foreigners falls below that of later times, we have our Lord's authority for admitting that O. T. legislation made concessions to the hardness of Jewish hearts (Matt. xix. 8). Summaries of the moral requirements of Jehovah are found in the Decalogue (Exod. xx.), the Book of the Covenant (xxi.-xxiii.), and the law of holiness (Lev. xvii.-xxvi.); and the subject is further illustrated by such pictures as those of the righteous man in Job xxix., and the virtuous woman in Prov. xxxi. 10-31. A representative passage is

Ezek. xviii. 5-9, "But if a man be just and do that which is lawful and right, and hath not eaten upon the mountain"—*i.e.*, engaged in forbidden and possibly idolatrous rites—" neither hath lifted up his eyes to the idols of the house of Israel, nor defiled his neighbour's wife, nor come near to a woman in her separation; and hath not wronged any, but hath restored to the debtor his pledge, hath spoiled none by violence, hath given his bread to the hungry, and hath covered the naked with a garment; he that hath not given forth upon usury, nor taken interest; that hath withdrawn his hand from iniquity, hath executed true judgment between man and man, hath walked in My statutes, and hath kept My judgments, to deal truly: he is just and shall surely live, saith the Lord Jehovah." This description of the just man, with its combination of ritual and morality, of positive and negative virtue, corresponds very fairly to the general tenor of O. T. teaching as to conduct. It is often said that O. T. righteousness is unduly negative, a view perhaps largely based upon the "thou shalt nots" of the Decalogue, but this objection is not sustained by an exhaustive examination.

Moreover, O. T. righteousness is by no means confined to external conduct, it extends also to character and motive. Hatred, envy, malice, and covetousness are denounced, and the Israelite is "to love his neighbour" as himself (Lev. xix. 18). He is moreover to love God with all his heart and soul and might, and to keep His commandments in his heart (Deut. vi. 5). Trust or faith in God, reverence, godly fear, humility, and gratitude are constantly inculcated. Meekness or humility ('anawa) is especially singled out in the later literature as a characteristic virtue of the true believer.

The O. T. ideal of righteousness is most concisely expressed in the words of Micah vi. 8: "He hath showed thee, O man, what is good: and what doth the Lord require of thee, but to do justly, and love mercy, and walk humbly with thy God."

28. **Sin.**—All sin is essentially disobedience to God, transgression of His commandments, failure to conform to the divine standard of righteousness. Sin may be regarded from different points of view, and sins may be divided into several classes. There are various terms for sin, sinful, and to sin, corresponding to these classes and points of view: *ra'* (E.V., "evil") is used in a perfectly general sense, like the Eng. equivalent; *het, hattath, hatta'a* (E.V., "sin") regard sin as a missing of the mark, or of the right way, the opposite of a straight (*yashar*) course of conduct; *rasha'* (E.V., "wicked") is used of those who do not conform to the divine law, the class contrasted with the "righteous," *çaddiq*; the cognate nouns denote the quality of such sin, and the verb *hirshia'* denotes "declare guilty," in opposition to, *hiçdiq*, "declare innocent": *pesha'* (E.V., "transgression") denotes rebellion against God; *'awon* (E.V., "iniquity") like *het* originally denoted crooked conduct, and came to be used of guilt or a state of sinfulness. These and similar terms emphasise the essential characteristics of sin—disobedience, and hostility to God.

Other terms regard sin as ignorance and foolishness. In Isa. v. 13, and Hosea iv. 6, it is the lack of knowledge which has involved Israel in ruinous sin. Accordingly the sinner is constantly spoken of as *nabal*, "fool," and sin as *nebala*, "folly." Similarly sin is empty and futile, *'awen* (E.V., "iniquity") nothingness; and essentially false. Such ignorance and folly issue in pride—a sin upon which the O. T. frequently dwells, providing distinct terms for its several varieties—and in mocking, scornful contempt for God and His faithful servants. The *leç* (E.V., "scorner") is the standing title of the sinner in Proverbs.

Other terms, again, regard sin as wrong done to man, especially *hamas* (E.V., "violence.") Under this head come the terms for the various offences against social order and decency, murder, theft, fraud, adultery, and other sexual crimes, false witness and other forms of lying, and cruelty.

Moreover sin, like righteousness, is a quality of character as well as conduct; many of the above terms—*e.g.*, pride, folly, etc., apply to inner disposition as well as to external acts. Persistent sinfulness is spoken of as a hardening or stubbornness of the heart.

From the point of view of the ritual, sins are classed as (*a*) "hidden sins," done through inadvertence, for which ritual atonement could be made; and (*b*) presumptuous or deliberate sins, for which no such atonement was possible.*

29. Rewards and Punishments.—Without attempting any formal statement of the relations of human freedom and divine sovereignty, O. T. always takes

---

* For a full statement of the various terms for sin and sins, see Schultz, ii., 281; Oehler, i., 231.

for granted the responsibility of man for his actions, and teaches that righteousness will be rewarded and sin punished. As the O. T. deals almost exclusively with the present life, these rewards and punishments mostly take the form of material loss or prosperity, a failure of crops or fertility, poverty or wealth, sickness or health, defeat or victory, a short or long life, childlessness or a large family. Yet many passages describe the highest good as fellowship with God and the sense of His approval, and regard the loss of these blessings as the severest punishment. Hence sometimes temporal misfortunes are deplored, not so much on account of physical pain and material loss, as because they are regarded as signs of the divine displeasure.

30. Forgiveness. Minor sins were forgiven on condition of the offering of suitable sacrifices; such rites involved confession, and doubtless implied repentance and amendment. The Levitical law does not provide any atonement for deliberate and heinous sins. Similarly many passages in the prophets declare that Israel and Judah are beyond forgiveness and must be cut off. In the latter case, however, sin is unpardonable because of persistence in exceptional wickedness. On the other hand, the doctrine of the restoration of Israel and Judah implies that even such punishment is not final, the nation survives its ruin and rises again from its ashes. Thus we obtain a cycle of sin, punishment, ruin, forgiveness, restoration, which illustrates the ancient Israelite doctrine that sin is atoned for by punishment, and does not finally alienate from God; thus if the sinner ceases to persist in his wickedness, he may, after due punishment, be restored to favour with God. So in Isa. xl. 2, Jerusalem is forgiven when she has received at the hand of Jehovah double for all her sins. This is represented in the Levitical law by its treatment of venial sins. In the history, Moses is punished for his pride in striking of the rock, David for the murder of Uriah, and Manasseh for his apostasy, but even these heinous sins do not finally exclude from forgiveness. In such cases forgiveness is in no way connected with any ritual observances. Such examples and teaching intimate that no sin, however grievous, irrevocably withdraws the nation or the individual from the grace of Jehovah. The conditions of forgiveness are, therefore, for venial sins, the absence of deliberate intent, confession, repentance, amendment and the observance of prescribed ritual. In the case of heinous sins, the offender may be punished with death, and so pass beyond the range of the O. T. teaching as to forgiveness; but even heinous sins may be forgiven, after punishment, if the sinner repents and amends his life.

Two passages, however, transcend these doctrines. In Isa. liii. the vicarious sufferings of the Righteous One secure forgiveness for sinners. In Ezek. xxxvi. 25, 26, repentance and amendment appear as the result of forgiveness: as in Rom. ii. 4, "the goodness of God leadeth thee to repentance" (cf. Wisdom xi. 23).

31. Spiritual Gifts.—In spite of the theoretic sanctity of Israel, religion always found the individual burdened with guilt and under the influence of sinful propensities. Its first task was to lead him to repentance and amendment, and then to foster and develop his righteousness. As one instrument in such operations the O. T. recognises the free activity of the human will; it constantly appeals to man to repent and amend, and therefore assumes that he is able to do so—*e.g.*, Ezek. xviii. 30, 31, " Repent and turn from all your transgressions; so iniquity shall not be your ruin. Cast away from all your transgressions, wherein ye have transgressed; and make you a new heart and a new spirit; for why will ye die, O house of Israel?" Thus, from one point of view, repentance is an act of the human will, whose freedom itself is ultimately a divine gift. Yet from another point of view, it is Jehovah who gives His people one heart and one way that they may fear Him for ever, and puts His fear in their hearts that they may not depart from Him for ever (Jer. xxxii. 39, 40). The spiritual act which combines human volition and divine working is faith, in which man yields himself to the redeeming and regenerating influence of God. The familiar attitudes ascribed to the believer in the O. T. of trusting in Jehovah and in His word, of waiting and hoping for His salvation, imply a dependence on, and surrender to, the will of God, which are the essence of that faith, through which divine grace controls the soul. The revelation of God to Israel, His dealings with His people, and the divinely appointed ordinances of Israelite religion all served to inspire the believer with faith, hope, and love towards Jehovah.

32. Apparent Failure of Divine Justice.—This is the great theme of O. T. speculation, the difficulty which drove inspired men to the verge of scepticism, and even seemed to place them in antagonism to the very axioms of O. T. revelation. Their discussions dealt with a very limited and special aspect of the general problem of the origin and existence of material and moral evil. Moral evil in men, possibly also in supernatural beings, was accepted as a fact, without any serious attempt (cf. § 34) to explain its origin or reconcile its existence with the moral government of God. God was recognised as the author of material evil, and as prosperity and success were the rewards of virtue, so suffering was the punishment of sin. Hence, a doctrine of suffering prevailed which might be formulated thus: As all virtue is rewarded by corresponding blessings, so all sin is punished by an accurately adjusted amount of suffering. A logic, which was perhaps technically accurate, drew the further conclusion that all prosperity is the reward and token of virtue, and all suffering is the just penalty of some present or previous sin. This proposition is insisted on by Job's friends, and is confirmed in the epilogue to Job, in which his integrity is manifested by his restoration to more than his former prosperity. Similarly in Psalm lxvi. 18, the Psalmist is convinced of his innocence, not because he has a clear conscience, but because his prayer has been answered; if he had regarded iniquity in his heart the Lord would not have heard him, but God had heard him.

The difficulties of such a theory were aggravated for the Israelite by the limited range of his speculations on divine retribution. For him the divine rewards of conduct chiefly consisted of prosperity, a long life, a large and prosperous family. Under such circumstances, very slight observation and experience showed that, *primâ facie*, facts did not bear out the theory. The wicked flourished, the righteous came to ruin. How then was it possible to "justify the ways of God to man"?

The difficulty existed, in some measure, even in regard to the nation. National prosperity did not always vary directly with national righteousness, and, especially after the return, Israel often felt itself an innocent sufferer at the hands of powerful and prosperous nations of inferior religion and morality. The difficulty admitted of two explanations: the nation might be suffering for the sins of individuals, like Achan, or, for the sins of its forefathers. Future salvation and prosperity might redress the balance, exhibit the even justice of God, and justify Israel to the world. This problem, however, peculiarly concerned the individual, who looked for the just reward of his conduct and the vindication of his character within the narrow limits of an earthly life. For him the difficulty often became a constant and intolerable burden, and O. T. theology wrestled with this problem for its very existence.

Naturally the formal discussion of the problem does not make its appearance in literature in the earliest days of the history of Israel. Indeed, at all times, and especially in the dawn of religion, the sense of the impenetrable mystery of the divine character and dealings prevented men from appreciating the logical consequences of a belief in the moral nature of God.

Thus the speeches of the Almighty in the Book of Job appeal to the self-distrustful reverence which shrinks from measuring God by the footrule of the human understanding. Yet the Holy Spirit does not allow men to rest in blind submission to apparent injustice, but ever arouses them afresh to an inspired curiosity, or even scepticism, that prepares the way for further revelation. Accordingly O. T. returns again and again to the discussion of this perpetual question.

One partial solution was suggested by another aspect of the mystery of the divine will. Man has only a very imperfect knowledge of the absolute or divine standard of morality. "Who can understand his errors?" "I know nothing against myself; yet am I not hereby justified: but He that judgeth me is the Lord." All men are guilty of unconscious sins, which are "hidden" alike from themselves and their neighbours. Many acts that seem innocent to men may be sinful in the eyes of God. Thus the suffering of an apparently innocent man might be due to such unconscious sins. We have seen that much of the ritual provides for the expiation of such sins. Obviously, however, this solution could not be more than partial. If consistently applied—as for instance to all the sufferings of the righteous—it involved a belief that divine and human morality were altogether different; this would have destroyed the influence of moral motives and encouraged superstition and magic. The divine will cannot be a moral standard for men unless they know it, and responsibility is limited by the extent to which it can be known.

Another partial explanation was derived from the fact that the suffering of the righteous and the prosperity of the wicked were often transient, and each received before his death the due reward of his works. Attempts were sometimes made to solve the problem by suggesting that this always happened. Job's sufferings are compensated for—in the epilogue —by a long period of renewed prosperity. Psalm after psalm rejoices in the prospect that the wicked will be punished and the righteous delivered :
" Mark the perfect man, and behold the upright :
For the latter end of that man is peace ;
As for transgressors, they shall be destroyed together.
The latter end of the wicked shall be cut off" (Psalm xxxvii. 37, 38). In Psalm lxxiii. 19 the believer, perplexed at the prosperity of the wicked considers " their latter end"; he goes into the sanctuary and perceives that destruction will come suddenly upon them. But this explanation again could only be partial. The righteous often perished in their misery and the wicked died in a prosperous old age, filled with treasure, satisfied with children, leaving the rest of their substance to their babes (Psalm xvii. 14).

Resort was also had to an invariable expedient in such controversies ; apologists ventured to deny the facts in the interests of dogma. They maintained that the sufferings of ostensibly good men were due to conscious sins done in secret. When loss or sickness, bereavement or early death befell the seemingly righteous man, he was thereby clearly shown to be a hypocrite. The speeches of Job's friends and of Elihu are largely devoted to the exposition of this argument. It must have been impossible to make any universal application of the corresponding principle to the prosperity of the wicked, but all analogy suggests that much may have been accomplished in this direction also, and that the vices of prosperity were often condoned or even regarded as virtues. The Chronicler ignores the vices of ancient kings like David and Solomon, whose reigns had been splendid and glorious. Though this principle might sometimes afford a true explanation, yet on the whole it was utterly demoralising; it tended to destroy all faith in human nature, and it could seldom satisfy the sufferer or his real friends. If the sufferer accepted the doctrine that his misery was a proof of his sin, he was betrayed into the hypocrisy of stultifying his own conscience.

These explanations only tended to deny or minimise the difficulty; the problem remained unsolved. The moral government of God was asserted throughout, and the failure to reconcile it with facts continually threw men back on the mystery of the divine dealings, as in the Book of Job.

Two principles, however, stand out from these discussions, and seem to have mitigated the stress upon human faith: these are vicarious atonement, and the spiritual character of true blessedness.

Vicarious suffering was involved in the moral discipline of Israel. By an anticipation of the solidarity of humanity, O. T. taught that the nation as a whole suffered for the sins of individuals, the innocent with and for the guilty. Israel was defeated before Ai on account of Achan's sin, and David's wickedness in taking a census was expiated by the death of seventy thousand of his innocent subjects. There might, of course, be individual exceptions from national ruin. Lot was rescued from Sodom—where, however, he was merely a resident alien—and Baruch and Ebedmelech were promised personal safety in the ruin of Jerusalem. On the other hand, according to Gen. xviii. 32, the virtue of ten righteous men would avail to save a guilty city. Nine such, apparently, must perish with their guilty kinsfolk. Moreover, the continuity of the nation involved the punishment of one generation for the sins of its predecessors. The captivity was regarded as a punishment of Manasseh's apostasy. The guilt of Saul's bloody house was expiated by the execution of his seven sons and grandsons. Ahab and Hezekiah were condemned to suffer in the person of their descendants. On the other hand, here also, the vicarious influence of suffering and action has its positive side, God bears with David's dynasty, for the sake of their great ancestor. The positive and negative aspects are summed up in the statement that God punishes the children for their father's sins unto three or four generations, but shows mercy unto the children of the righteous for a thousand generations (Exod. xx. 5, 6; cf. Psalm lxxix. 8). But Ezek. xviii. states expressly that the righteous son shall not die for his father's sin, nor the wicked son be saved by his father's righteousness. The affirmation and the denial of hereditary responsibility express two truths which are complementary not contradictory.

Thus, through the solidarity and continuity of the family and nation, O. T. theology recognised the principle of the innocent suffering for the guilty; and in Isa. liii. this principle is adopted to explain the sufferings of the righteous. Such vicarious suffering is not a useless sacrifice, but ministers to the need of the guilty, and may even win their forgiveness. The national unity of Israel, by which the innocent suffered for his guilty kinsfolk, answers to that solidarity of humanity by which the death of Christ avails for the race.

The second principle was that of the spiritual character of true blessedness. Much of the difficulty as to God's moral government arose out of the close identification of His rewards with material benefits. This high estimate of external prosperity is thoroughly discredited by Ecclesiastes, which shows that health and riches, long life and a large family, may be—or, acccording to it, are—" vanity of vanities," " vanity and vexation of spirit," no blessings at all. His reasoning obviously leads up to a conclusion which he does not state—namely, that such vanities cannot be infallible tokens of man's spiritual state or of God's favour. On the other hand the Psalter shows that men could find delight in fellowship with God and have assurance of His approval, even when poor and oppressed. "If only I have Thee I ask for nothing else in earth or heaven; though body and soul perish, yet Thou, O God, art my soul's comfort and my portion for ever" (Psalm lxxiii. 25, 26). (Smend 453.)

No longer crushed by the delusion that suffering

was merely a token of God's wrath, man discerned its disciplinary value :
"It is good for me that I have been afflicted ;
That I might learn Thy statutes " (Psa. cxix. 71).
The discussion of this problem naturally involved occasional reference to the hope of a future life (see next section), and the suggestion that some light may be thrown on the problem by the possibilities of the future state. But such suggestions are rare and never clearly formulated, no one ventured to call in the new world to redress the balance of the old. Dan. xii. 2, 3, does not allude to our problem. Perhaps this reticence was not wholly due to uncertainty about man's future life. Since eternal life has been included in our speculations on the apparent moral discrepancy between the actual state of the universe and the character of its Author and Ruler, the problem has not been solved, it has only become more complicated and assumed larger dimensions.

33. The Future Life.—O. T. contains very little explicit statement as to the future life. The state or place of the dead is known as Sheol, probably the "Hollow Place" (cf. "hell," "Hölle") ; and more rarely as Abaddon, the "Place of Destruction." It is nowhere said that death is the termination of conscious life, and even necromancy implies a belief in continued existence after death. But Sheol, like Hades, is a realm of shadowy, impotent ghosts, and existence in Sheol seems conceived as a kind of vague nightmare (cf. the scene of the dead kings and nations in Sheol in Isa. xiv., Ezek. xxxii.). According to Eccles. ix. 10, "there is no work, nor device, nor knowledge, nor wisdom, in Sheol." In the same spirit, the inhabitants of Sheol are called Rephaim, "the feeble ones."

Such conceptions of life in Sheol were very far removed from that future life which N. T. describes as beginning with the resurrection; but the teaching of O. T. partly bridges the gulf between the two. The first suggestions of such a resurrection are met with in connection with the nation, and its repretatives, patriarchs, and prophets. The narratives of the translation of Enoch and Elijah indicate a belief in a possibility of a future life of bliss with God. The possibility of release from Sheol is implied in the accounts of how Elisha raised the son of the Shunammite from the dead, and of how the prophet's bones revived a corpse. With regard to the nation, as a rule the prophets teach that the new Israel will spring from the surviving remnant of the old. Yet sometimes they seem to intimate that the expansion of the remnant into a numerous people is not to be brought about by any tedious process of natural increase of population, but by a kind of resurrection of the ancient people. So Hosea vi. 2: "After two days He will revive us: on the third day He will raise us up, and we shall live before Him"; and in Ezek. xxxvii. 1-14, the new Israel is formed by the revivifying of the dry bones of dead Israelites. The nation even involves its Redeemer in its own fortunes, and in Isa. liii., the Righteous Servant accomplishes His mission by His death and resurrection.

Such instances of individual or national resurrection readily suggest the principle of a general resurrection of mankind. But this further step was taken with much hesitation. Even the discussion of the divine allotment of happiness and suffering to individuals barely hinted at possible readjustment and compensation hereafter. We find the hope rather than the assurance of such vindication of the divine righteousness, and that only in a few passages. In Job xiv. 13, 14, the sufferer even ventures to hope that he may be recalled to life from Sheol; and in spite of corrupt text and doubtful translation (xix. 25, 26), "I know that my Redeemer liveth," etc., seems to intimate a similar vision (cf. also Psalms xi. 7, xvii. 15).

It is only in Dan. xii. 2 that we are told that "many of them that sleep in the dust of the earth shall awake, some to everlasting life, and some to shame and everlasting contempt."

DIVISION II

GOD AND THE UNIVERSE

DIVISION II

GOD AND THE UNIVERSE

34. Man.—Israel is always the main interest, as well as the starting point, of O. T. theology. Yet, if to understand the " flower in the crannied wall, what it is, root and all, and all in all," is to know " what God and man is," a similar understanding of the purpose and operation of the divine dealings with Israel would illuminate the whole range of theology. Israel stood related to the human race; to be thoroughly effective the God of Israel must control the mutual relations of Israel and mankind—*i.e.*, He must be the Lord of nations. The question of the relation of God to the heathen naturally arose from the relation of Israel to its neighbours. Its God, in the first instance met the heathen as its champion against its enemies. A champion, however, is not always victorious. Heathen, and popular Jewish theology could imagine the divine champion of one nation defeated by the gods of its enemies; and it was understood that in a national defeat the national deity might be included among the vanquished. Thus the victories of Israel implied Jehovah's power over vanquished gods and nations. But the prophets even discerned the outstretched arm of Jehovah in the catastrophes of His people. Their conquerors, Egypt, Assyria, and Babylon, were the instruments of His justice. Hence the whole course of history manifested the supremacy of Jehovah over all mankind. Thus, too, the Jewish conceptions of the power and majesty of Jehovah became more exalted as their international horizon widened.

But in spite of the Israelite standpoint of the O. T. its recognition of the moral character of Jehovah excluded the possibility of arbitrary favouritism. God overthrows heathen empires on account of their sins, and not merely to serve the interests of Israel. Amongst their sins are reckoned their mutual injustice and their treatment of their own subjects, as well as the injuries inflicted upon Israel. Jehovah is interested in justice, benevolence, and good government amongst all mankind.

This attitude is implied by the genealogies; all mankind—and not merely the Israelites—are made in the divine image and likeness, and share the life which Jehovah breathed into the nostrils of the first man. All existing races have a share in the deliverance from the Flood and the covenant with Noah. Moreover, Ishmael and Esau, Moab and Ammon, inherit divine promises as well as Israel.

O. T. too, recognises genuine religion quite independent of the revelation made to Israel. Melchisedek king of Salem, priest of El Elyon (E.V., "the Most High God") receives tithes from Abraham and is recognised in Psalm cx. as the highest type of priest; Jethro, the priest of Midian, is exhibited in the most favourable and honourable light; and the Mesopotamian Balaam becomes the organ of divine revelation. Moreover, the Law is not unmindful of the resident alien (*ger.*). He may become circumcised, partake of the Passover, and thus virtually become an Israelite, or more strictly a proselyte (Exod. xii. 48).

O. T. constantly recognises God's interest in the heathen. Hence Jonah's mission to Nineveh, and the flattering picture of the Moabite widow, Ruth. In Amos ix. 7, God's interest in the Philistines and the Syrians is placed on the same level as His care for Israel; and in Isa. xl.-lxvi., Israel's mission is to be a light to lighten the Gentiles. In Daniel, other nations have their guardian angels as well as Israel; and Deut. iv. 19 states that Jehovah assigned the host of heaven as objects of worship to all the nations under the whole heaven. But whatever traces there may be in the O. T. of divine recognition of worship, outside the religion of Israel, such recognition is only temporary and provisional. As the starting point of humanity is its creation in the image of God, so the goal is its comprehension in that Kingdom of God, which also realises the highest hopes of Israel.

There is, therefore, no absolute anthropology in the O. T.; man's relation to God is mediated from beginning to end through the Chosen People. Strictly speaking the O. T. has no doctrine of man as man, but only as Israelite. Adam and the patriarchs owe their religious status to the fact that they are to be the ancestors of Israel, they are not mere men but the elect subjects of special covenants, and represent Israel and not ordinary humanity. On the other hand so far as the true Israel is ultimately to embrace all mankind, Israel and the religious life of Israel become the types of humanity and its relation to God. Man, therefore, is a responsible, free agent, capable by his spirit (*ruaḥ*) of having fellowship with God, and of receiving or resisting the suggestions of the Spirit of God (cf. pp. 71, 105, 112, 176, 178, 187).

35. Evil.—O. T. offers no explanation of the origin or existence of evil, especially of moral evil. Isa. xlv. 6, 7 indeed states: "I am Jehovah and there is none else. I form the light and create darkness; I make peace and create evil: I Jehovah do all these things." But the inspired writer is here emphasising the divine unity and not seeking to explain the mystery of evil; he is probably thinking rather of suffering than of sin. On the other hand, according to Gen. i., "God saw all that He had made and it was very good." The document to which Gen. i. belongs states in Gen. vi. 11, 12, that the earth became corrupt, but it does not explain how a perfect creation fell from its primeval purity. But although Gen. iii. comes originally from a different document, the author of the Pentateuch may have intended it to account for this lapse. According to Gen. iii., sin in the human race had its origin in external suggestion, to which first woman and then man succumbed. But the narrative throws no light on the origin of evil, for we find it already existing in a most malignant form in the serpent, which is itself a creature of God, and which —if we connect with Gen i.—had been pronounced very good.

O. T. as a whole assumes moral evil and human responsibility, but makes no attempt to explain them, or to reconcile them with God's sovereignty and perfect moral nature.

36. Material Universe.—If Jehovah was to be in any real sense God, even of Israel, He must not only be Lord of the Nations, but also of the Universe. His lordship of the nations involved His supremacy over the lands they inhabited. He sent pestilence and famine upon the heathen as well as upon His own people. Moreover, in blessing Israel with fertility or afflicting it with barrenness, heaven and all its hosts were His instruments. Thus Jehovah is Creator and Ruler alike of earth and heaven. At the same time the problems of the origin of matter, or of an absolute beginning of things, do not seem to have presented themselves to O. T. writers. When God created (Gen. i.) *bara'*, earth and heaven, the prior existence of a waste abyss seems implied, and there is no sufficient evidence that the mere term *bara'* proves that a creation out of nothing is intended.

Similarly O. T. has no fixed and definite doctrine of the ultimate destiny of the present material universe. Many passages, however, suggest that one of the preliminaries to the establishment of the Kingdom of God will be the complete transfiguration of the present material universe or even its destruction (Isa. li. 6, lxvi. 22, lxv. 17 ; Joel ii. 30, 31 ; Haggai ii. 21).

37. Supernatural Beings.—The lordship of Jehovah over earth and heaven implies His supremacy in the spiritual universe. Here, too, O. T. starts from the conception of a national deity. Such a God to be all-availing must be supreme over all other gods. As champion of Israel He must be able to subdue the supernatural powers which fight for their enemies. He can only secure fertility for His land by controlling the spirits of the heavenly bodies, to whom the heathen ascribed an independent deity. Eastern imagination peopled the springs, and ancient trees, the stones, cairns, and hill tops with innumerable spirits, able to ban or bless their human neighbours. The Israelite lived in continual fear for himself, his family, his cattle and farm, unless he was assured that these spirits were also subject to the will of the God of Israel.

The divine name which Jehovah bears as one of a class of spiritual or supernatural beings is *ELOHIM*. Elohim is also used of the gods of the heathen, of the spirit of the dead prophet Samuel, and even of exalted earthly authorities. When it is desired to call attention to the fact that the True God is referred to, *ha-Elohim, the* God is often used.

The form is plural, and when it is used of false gods, etc., it may be construed either as a singular or plural, but when it refers to the True God, it is almost always construed as a singular. O. T. does not explain why the plural is used. It has been held to indicate the exaltation and infinite variety of the divine qualities and operations—plural of majesty —or as a relic of a time when the supernatural world was conceived of as a plurality of undistinguished beings—Elohim.

We find traces in O. T. of various views of the relation of other supernatural beings to Jehovah.

i. According to the ordinary Semitic view, to which popular Jewish superstition long tended to return, Jehovah, Chemosh, Moloch, etc., etc., were each of them tribal gods, of the same genus, but differing in power and authority.

ii. There was also a tendency to confuse Jehovah with other gods. He seems sometimes to have been worshipped as Baal or Moloch.

iii. While the heathen gods are still recognised as actual supernatural beings, Jehovah is regarded as a being of a different order, unique and supreme (Isa. xl., etc.).

iv. The heathen gods are regarded as NO-gods, nonentities ('*ELILIM*, not '*ELOHIM*).

v. In Daniel the heathen gods are replaced by guardian angels of heathen nations.

By these steps Jehovah's rivals were reduced either to nonentities or to His humble servants, and took their place in His heavenly court, amongst the various orders and species of angels. Thus Jehovah is shown to be unique and supreme amongst supernatural beings.

38. The Doctrine of God.—We have already mentioned the names, Jehovah, etc., which are personal to the God of Israel, and Elohim which describes God as a supernatural being. Besides these *EL* is a divine name common to all Semitic languages. It is of uncertain origin, often explained as the "Strong One," and sometimes supposed to be etymologically connected with Elohim. '*ELOAH* is merely a singular formed from Elohim, and chiefly occurs in Job. 'EL 'ELYON, in Gen. xiv. is the deity worshipped by Melchisedeck. Elsewhere, 'ELYON (E.V., "Most High") is an epithet or name of the God of Israel; it is also a Phœnician divine name. SHADDAI, also in EL SHADDAI (E.V., "Almighty"), is a name of uncertain origin and meaning.

We may now briefly summarise what is stated or implied in O. T. concerning the doctrine of God. The most formal statements on the subject are Isa. xl.-xlviii.

He is *Elohim*, a supernatural being, differing in undefined and undefinable ways from men. In spite of the plural form of *Elohim*, He is One, unique amongst, and supreme over, all other supernatural beings, or *Elohim*. He is therefore self-existent and self-sufficient, according to the interpretation attached in Exod. iii. 14, to the personal name Jehovah, "I am that I am." * He is personal, all personal attributes, consciousness, will, emotion, are freely ascribed to Him.

Positively God is the origin of all things, the Creator of the universe and of mankind. He is omnipotent, omniscient, omnipresent and eternal. Negatively, He is subject to no limitations. As omnipotent He is unlimited either by the forces or qualities of matter.

* The alternative explanations : "I become what I become," "I will be what I will be," do not materially affect the general testimony of the interpretation to the divine uniqueness and self-sufficiency.

GOD AND THE UNIVERSE

The absolute freedom of God's action in nature is shown by miracles, extraordinary and surprising deviations from what is familiar to man's experience of Nature (*pele niphla'oth mopheth*), which serve as signs (*'oth*), and also show that He is not limited by the will of animals, men, or supernatural beings. As omniscient, He is not limited by distance in space, by the past or future in time, by intervening material obstacles, or by the privacy of human consciousness. He "declareth unto man what is his thought" (Amos iv. 13). As omnipresent He can manifest Himself, speak, act, everywhere, in Egypt and Chaldea, as well as in Palestine; His special connection with Palestine is not due to any necessity of His own nature, but to His free election of Israel. Thus Psalm cxxxix. 8-12:

> " If I ascend up into heaven, Thou art there,
> If I make my bed in Sheol, behold, Thou art there.
> If I take the wings of the morning,
> And dwell in the uttermost parts of the sea;
> Even there shall Thy hand lead me,
> And Thy right hand shall hold me.
> If I say, surely the darkness shall overwhelm me,
> And the light about me shall be night;
> Even the darkness hideth not from Thee,
> But the night shineth as the day;
> The darkness and the light are both alike to Thee."

He is eternal, the O. T. knows nothing of any beginning

or ending of God, but always states or implies His existence before all things, during all history, and beyond its farthest outlook into the future.

In His relation to mankind, as typified by His dealings with Israel (cf. § 33), He shows Himself a moral being, self-consistent, just and benevolent. Thus, in Exod. xxxiv. 5-7, He proclaims "His Name" as "Jehovah, Jehovah, a God full of compassion and gracious, slow to anger, and plenteous in mercy and truth, keeping mercy for a thousand generations, forgiving iniquity and transgression and sin; and that will by no means clear the guilty; visiting the iniquity of the fathers upon the children, and the children's children, upon the third and fourth generation."

www.ingramcontent.com/pod-product-compliance
Lightning Source LLC
Chambersburg PA
CBHW031833230426
43669CB00009B/1333